Endorsements

When I think about my friend James Goll, I think of a man without compromise, a man without guile. His pursuit of all that is true seems to attract insights and revelation that is not normal for most of us. James Goll's passion is to make it practical, and then give it all away. I believe *The Discerner* is a gift from this prophet to the church. And much like his book *The Seer*, it will mark the church for decades to come. Enjoy, and be inspired, equipped, and empowered *for such a time as this*.

- *Bill Johnson*
  Bethel Church, Redding, CA
  Author, *When Heaven Invades Earth* and *God is Good*

The number one weapon the devil deploys in the last days isn't the mark of the beast, radical Islam, or a nuclear holocaust. His number one weapon is deception. If his number one weapon is deception, the number one gift most needed (and most frequently absent) in the body of Christ is—the discerning of spirits! James does a masterful job of detailing how you can surrender all your senses to the Holy Spirit so you can see, hear, feel, taste, smell and know—with a deep inner knowing—the Spirit of God. He also exposes the spirit of deception and how it operates, outlining the traps and influences it uses to try to set you up for offense or error. James is an experienced guide and teacher...the ability to discern truth and discern error is the path that leads you into the "all" that God has planned for your life.

- *Lance Wallnau*
  Founder, Lance Learning Group
  Author, *God's Chaos Candidate: Donald J. Trump and the American Unraveling*

I just finished James Goll's *The Discerner*, and—wow! Let me say it this way: there are many resources about hearing God's voice, but this goes way deeper, gifting you from the riches of James' life experience and prophetic ministry. It gives you a road map for navigating how to manifest the revelation you receive, and letting God change your very nature in the process. James is an encyclopedia of revelation and supernatural materials, and this is like a capstone of all his previous wonderful works on revelatory gifting. I highly recommend it!

- *Shawn Bolz*
  www.bolzministries.com

James is such an immense treasure trove of wisdom and revelation on everything to do with spiritual seeing and discerning. No matter what level of discernment you presently have, this will provide an upgrade to the next level. The lessons on your spiritual senses are priceless. It is all connected to growing in intimacy with God—and that will be the fruit.

- *Johnny Enlow*
  International speaker and author, *The Seven Mountain Renaissance*

One of the greatest gifts God has given to His people is the gift of discernment. How we need wise, compassionate discernment in these last days! In *The Discerner*, James Goll lays out before us a clear and concise teaching on having a heart to discern the works of God and the deeds of the enemy. I've not read a better book for preparing us for the days to come. The ones who discern the ways of God will be the ones to lead us into the coming glory. Every pastor, leader, intercessor, and worshipper must read this book. Every believer will be built up and given tools to be a valuable discerner in the days ahead. Buy one for yourself and one for a friend. They will thank you for it!

- *Brian Simmons*
  Stairway Ministries
  Lead translator, The Passion Translation Project

Dr. James Goll is one of God's chosen and anointed vessels to identify prophets and to grow the prophetic gifts and abilities within the body of Christ. He has skillfully taught and mentored on various aspects of prophetic revelation over the years, and now he introduces a very important component: *The Discerner*. There is very little written about this subject, and yet it is vital for us to understand…a remarkable work that will continue to teach and train others for generations to come. Well done!

- *Patricia King*
  Founder, Patricia King Ministries
  www.xpministries.com

As I travel the nation teaching spiritual warfare principles, one truth becomes painfully clear: the body of Christ, at large, lacks discernment. The reality is that many believers have simply not been activated or trained to discern spirits. Yet discernment is a vital gift in this hour as false prophets, false teachers, and even false christs are rising around the world with smooth sayings, rhymes and riddles. James Goll's *The Discerner* equips the body in discernment. Given the goings-on in the world and in the church, this is right on time…understand with clarity how to press into the gift of discernment to test the spirits.

- *Jennifer LeClaire*
  Senior Editor, *Charisma* and *SpiritLed Woman*
  Senior Leader, Awakening House of Prayer, Fort Lauderdale, FL

It would be difficult to imagine a time in which discernment was more important than now. James Goll has been an observer of, participant in, or leader of almost every important wave of the Holy Spirit in ministry for forty years and is perfectly suited to teach the church how to navigate the various competing moral, spiritual, and political paradigms in this modern world. *The Discerner* is full of rich insight and allows us to benefit from all that experience as he has watched and interacted with leaders, churches, denominations, and movements. You will gain a greater understanding of the forces that affect your life and how to intelligently maintain your walk with God.

- *Joan Hunter*
  Author and Healing Evangelist, Joan Hunter Ministries

The Discerner carries important truth and revelation that the Church desperately needs concerning discernment to detect and defeat the deception of the spirit of this age by tuning in to discern and hear the voice of truth from our Shepherd, Jesus. I recommend *The Discerner* as it will help readers understand how to cultivate a greater level of biblical discernment in general, as well as how to activate and grow in the gift of discernment in particular. Full of deep yet palatable revelation and practical teaching, I am sure that *The Discerner* will serve countless many as a beacon in the dark and a compass accurately pointing northward.

- *Apostle Guillermo Maldonado*
  King Jesus International Ministry, Miami, FL

With *The Seer*, James Goll delivered a groundbreaking book on the seer gift, releasing many into greater understanding, appreciation, and application of their anointing. Now, with *The Discerner*, James has again led us to another level of insight. When operating in the prophetic, there is the revelation, the interpretation, and the application of what has been revealed. The sharpening of our discernment takes us beyond just revelation to operating effectively in divine wisdom, which helps us not only perceive and receive from the Lord, but to practice and activate that prophetic wisdom with clarity. As believers, we cannot afford to live without the necessary discernment to distinguish between the voice of God, the voice of the enemy, and our own voice. *The Discerner* is a very timely work that will impart truth and bring instruction as to how we might have the mind of Christ (1 Corinthians 2:16) in every situation.

- *Dr. Ché Ahn*
  President, Harvest International Ministry
  Founding Pastor, HROCK Church, Pasadena, CA
  International Chancellor, Wagner University

I have known James Goll for over a decade. My friend and, even more, this friend of God is known for combining three strands of truth together in whatever he does. James brings a weight of scriptural teaching to produce a solid foundation. He then builds upon this by adding a second component of precedents found in Jewish and church history. This is followed by a third necessary ingredient of contemporary testimonies of the work of the Holy Spirit today. James has done it for us once again in *The Discerner*. What an excellent handbook to help believers in Messiah know how to live a supernatural life with effectiveness today.

- *Sid Roth*
  Host, *It's Supernatural!* TV
  Author, Evangelist and Inspirational Speaker

James Goll is not just a dear friend, I consider him to be one of profound mind and insight in relation to prophetic perception. As the Church continues to move forward into the intention of God for its future, more and more, you will be hearing of the need for a Pentecostal and Charismatic "Theology of Discernment". As people who believe in the fullness of the Spirit, our comprehension of the process of perception and discernment is influenced by our encounters with God the Father's three-fold cord that is never to be separated: The Holy Spirit, The Son of God, and The Scriptures. Within the interrelationship of the three, we as God's company of prophetic and kingly priests are coming to terms with how the entire purpose of discernment has to issue in godly responses and actions that bring about God's desired results. James' newest release, *The Discerner* gives us all a seat that the table where this conversation is taking place, and will continue to take place and expand as we move forward into the future Jesus has prepared for us.

- *Dr. Mark J. Chironna*
  Church On The Living Edge
  Mark Chironna Ministries
  Longwood, Florida

**GOD
ENCOUNTERS
MINISTRIES**
with James W. Goll

Published by
God Encounters Ministries
P.O. Box 1653, Franklin, TN 37065
www.godencounters.com

Copyright © 2017 James W. Goll
All rights reserved

Unless otherwise indicated, scripture is taken from the
New American Standard Bible®,
Copyright © 1960, 1962, 1963, 1968, 1971, 1972, 1973,
1975, 1977, 1995 by The Lockman Foundation
Used by permission. (www.Lockman.org)

As noted, scripture taken from the HOLY BIBLE, NEW INTERNATIONAL VERSION® (NIV)
Copyright © 1973, 1978, 1984 International Bible Society.
Used by permission of Zondervan. All rights reserved.

Scripture quotations marked (AMP) are taken from the Amplified Bible,
Copyright © 1954, 1958, 1962, 1964, 1965, 1987 by The Lockman Foundation.
Used by permission.

As noted, scripture taken from the King James Version (KJV)
The KJV is public domain in the United States.

All scripture is indicated by italics.

Classes and Other Resources

The following *The Discerner Study Guide* is great for individual study in your own home, with a small group, or in a classroom setting. It also serves as part of *The Discerner* class at God Encounters Ministries, along with *The Discerner* book and 12 Class Sessions taught by James W. Goll. Visit www.GodEncounters.com for more information about this and many other life-changing classes.

At the end of each detailed lesson are simple questions for your reflection and review. In the back of this study guide, you will find the answers to these questions to aid in your learning.

James W. Goll has many other resources available. They may be purchased at www.GodEncounters.com. For more information, visit our website, email info@godencounters.com or call 1-877-200-1604.

Dedication

As I prayed over the dedication for this particular study guide, two people came to my mind. Both of them have been friends and peers, and yet also spiritual leaders and advisers who have spoken into my life many times over many years.

In gratitude and as an act of honor, I wish to dedicate *The Discerner Study Guide* to the influential prophetess Cindy Jacobs and to Ché Ahn, one of the most significant apostles in this generation. Both of their lives have impacted me deeply, and I have needed and valued their discernment.

Thank you for investing in my life for so many years!

With Gratitude,

Dr. James W. Goll

Acknowledgments

Over the years, the Lord has graced me to walk with a company of people who have cheered for me, prayed for me, challenged me, and assisted me in many practical and spiritual ways. It has been said that a successful person surrounds himself with people with greater skills than he himself possesses. That is definitely true in my case. I want to acknowledge and honor a few of these stellar people who have helped me produce yet another study guide for your use.

I wish to thank the Staff and Board of God Encounters Ministries. You bring out the best in me and I am truly grateful! I have three board members who have been with me longer than I can remember: Dr. William (Bill) Greenman as Vice President, Dr. John Mark Rodgers as the Secretary of the Board and Elizabeth (Beth) Alves as a Director. For them, "thank you" is an inadequate statement for your years of faithfulness.

I would love to mention all the staff personnel who have worked with me over my 40 plus years in ministry. But that would be a very long list. But I do wish to acknowledge, the core of my current ministry staff—Jeffrey Thompson, Executive Director, Kay Durham, Financial Administrator, Don Clark, IT Director, Tyler Goll, Graphics Designer and Katie Sarvak, Executive Assistant—who have all also served me well for these many years, and their excellence and faithfulness mean the world to me.

May the Lord Bless Each One of You!

Dr. James W. Goll

Table of Contents

Introduction: Dropping the Plumb Line..15

SECTION ONE: RECEIVING REVELATION

Lesson One: Surrendering Your Senses to the Holy Spirit 19

Lesson Two: Seeing: You Have More than One Set of Eyes 27

Lesson Three: Hearing: Whatever He Hears, He Will Speak 35

Lesson Four: Feeling: From the Heart Flows the Issues of Life 43

Lesson Five: Tasting, Smelling & Other Leadings 51

Lesson Six: Knowing: The Sixth Sense..59

SECTION TWO: DISCERNING REVELATION

Lesson Seven: Testing the Spirits: Don't Believe Every Spirit!................69

Lesson Eight: The Spirit of Deception: Seductive and Manipulative......79

Lesson Nine: Exposing Demonic Influences: Setting the Captives Free ...87

Lesson Ten: Staying Out of Satan's Traps: Wisdom to Avoid Common Pitfalls 95

Lesson Eleven: Creating a Culture of Faith: Ingredients for a Safe House.............105

Lesson Twelve: Revelation's Ultimate Purpose: When the Word Becomes Flesh 115

Answers to the Reflection Questions 123

Recommended Reading 125

Additional Resources by James W. Goll 127

End Notes 129

Introduction: Dropping the Plumb Line

Back in Old Testament Judah, the prophet Amos started out as a nobody. He was not a priest or a member of a noble family; he herded sheep and tended sycamore fig trees. He never expected to hear God's voice, and he did not expect to become a prophet. But he applied himself to learning what he needed to know in order to be faithful to his prophetic calling:

"I was no prophet, nor was I a son of a prophet, but I was a sheep breeder and a tender of sycamore fruit. Then the LORD took me as I followed the flock, and the LORD said to me, "Go, prophesy to My people Israel." (Amos 7:14-15 NKJV). Amos obeyed, and he is best known for making public a word about how God was setting a "plumb line" in the nation of Israel to measure the truth and righteousness of the people and their rulers. The Spirit of God gave him this vision:

"The LORD was standing by a wall that had been built true to plumb, with a plumb line in his hand. And the LORD asked me, 'What do you see, Amos?' 'A plumb line,' I replied. Then the Lord said, 'Look, I am setting a plumb line among my people Israel; I will spare them no longer.'" (Amos 7:7-8 NIV). God's plumb line is all-important, not only for aligning crooked human life to His perfect uprightness, but also for discerning His voice in the first place. In the midst of all the noise of the world, we need to be able to distinguish God's voice clearly.

Like Amos, I work hard to bring a plumb line that can help the people of God do everything according to the word of the Lord. Whether I compose books or study guides, conduct seminars or lead prayer gatherings, I try to operate to the best of my ability according to what He has taught me. My primary resource, of course, is the Word of God, the Bible. But years of personal experience have made a huge difference in how I have learned to apply the Word. The Spirit is our best teacher, and in *The Discerner Study Guide* my desire is to bring you what I have learned from Him about receiving and discerning what God reveals to His people.

The twelve lessons contained in *The Discerner Study Guide* will take you on a journey of discovery. The first half of the study guide contains six revelatory lessons explaining how you can receive revelation from God by surrendering your natural senses. Then second half, lessons seven through twelve, help you bring the art of discernment right home. You will learn what to do when Satan tries to infiltrate God's message, and I will help you to create a lifestyle of faith that is healthy, balanced, dynamic and discerning.

In the final analysis, developing discernment is not as much about knowing the future as it is about bringing the kingdom of God to bear on the time and place in which you live. The gospel of John begins with the words, *"The Word became flesh and dwelt among us..., full of grace and truth"* (John 1:14), referring to the first coming of Jesus Christ.

In a very real way, you and I cause God's Word to dwell in the midst of the world as we remain sensitive to the flow of His Holy Spirit. Through our relationship with God, we receive revelation. And as we bring that revelation to the world around us, we actually incarnate His Word in very practical ways. Please join me in this "plumb line" course—*The Discerner Study Guide*. I want to pass on to you what has been passed down to me.

God Bless You Deeply!

James W. Goll

Section One:

Receiving Revelation

Lesson One:
Surrendering Your Senses to the Holy Spirit

I. **WHEN LIFE BECOMES "VIBRANT AND FULL OF COLOR"**

   A. **Hebrews 5:14 – Theme Scripture**
   "But solid food is for the mature, who because of practice have their senses trained to discern good and evil."

   B. **My Personal Experience: When Everything Became Vibrant**
   Years ago, my Christian life looked like our old black-and-white television. The programming and reception were not too bad, and I thought things were going along fine. Then everything shifted unexpectedly, and I have never wanted to go back.

   For some time, I had been getting various brief mental snapshots. I would notice something for a millisecond and think, "Where did that come from?" What was that? It was as if my senses were waking up. It was like beginning to see in color instead of in black-and-white. Or it was like growing out of being a baby, who drinks only milk, and beginning to sample solid food.

   C. **Believing for More**
   Do you want to stay on your current level or do you want to believe for more from the Lord? How do highly gifted and empowered believers do what they do? Faith is always the commodity needed to move progressively forward.

   D. **What Does "Solid Food Is for the Mature" Mean?**
   I have often pondered what the writer of the book of Hebrews meant when he stated, *"Solid food is for the mature."* I want to be mature, don't you? Some maturity comes from a thing called practice. But this I know for sure, to be mature means that you grow from one stage to the next.

II. **WHAT SENSES ARE WE TALKING ABOUT?**

   A. **This Is Something More than "Common Sense"**
   Sometimes when we read Hebrews 5:14, we automatically think of the phrase, "common sense." Is this what the writer of the Book of Hebrews meant or are there other senses to which this verse is referring?

B. We Each Have Five Natural Senses
1. Sight – Seeing with our Eyes
2. Hearing – Hearing with our Ears
3. Touch – Feeling with our skin
4. Taste – Tasting with our Tongue
5. Smell – Smelling with our Nose

C. Practice Sessions – There Is No Perfect Start!
Yes, practice does make perfect. Remember learning how to ride a bicycle? If you took a tumble and quit trying, then you would never have learned. So we must continually take practice sessions until our "training wheels" can been removed and we are able to glide with great joy.

D. Discern Both Good and Evil
Discernment involves discerning good and discerning evil, but many people find that they start out a lot better at one or the other. Maturity entails growth in both. We must learn to differentiate good from evil and evil from good, but we must grow in our capacities for discernment in both arenas—not just one.

III. THE NECESSITY OF PRESENTATION

A. From Romans 12:1-2
"Therefore I urge you, brethren, by the mercies of God to present your bodies a living and holy sacrifice, acceptable to God, which is your spiritual service of worship. And do not conform to this world, but be transformed by the renewing of your mind, so that you may prove what the will of God is, that which is good and acceptable and perfect."

B. From Romans 6:13, 19
"And do not go on presenting the members of your body to sin as instruments of unrighteousness to God... I am speaking in human terms because of the weakness of your flesh. For just as you presented your members as slaves to impurity and to lawlessness, so now present your members as slaves to righteousness, resulting in sanctification."

C. We Are a Triune Being: Spirit, Soul and Body
We are created in the image and likeness of God. There is only One God but expressed in three personages: God the Father, the Son and the Holy Spirit. So we are triune beings and comprised of these three equally important aspects.

D. Prayer of Presentation and Consecration
Pause right now, and in your own words from your heart, present the members of your body, the temple of God, to the Holy Spirit. Set your senses apart unto the Lord, realizing that to whomever you present yourself, to Him they become a slave. So, consecrate yourself and all six of your senses as instruments of righteousness in Jesus' name.

IV. THERE ARE A VARIETY OF GIFTS OF THE HOLY SPIRIT

A. From I Corinthians 12:4-7
"Now there are a variety of gifts, but the same Spirit. And there are a variety of ministries, and the same Lord. There are a variety of effects, but the same God who works all things in all persons. But to each one is given the manifestation of the Spirit for the common good."

B. From I Corinthians 12:8-11
"For to one is given the word of wisdom through the Spirit, and to another the word of knowledge according to the same Spirit; to another faith by the same Spirit, and to another gifts of healing by the one Spirit, and to another the effecting of miracles, and to another prophecy, and to another the distinguishing of spirits, to another various kinds of tongues, and to another the interpretation of tongues. But one and the same Spirit works all these things, distributing to each one individually just as He wills."

C. The Necessity of the Gift of Discerning of Spirits
In this study, we will major on the gift referred to above as "the distinguishing of spirits," or discernment. I suggest that the responsible exercise of any spiritual gift requires an ever-increasing degree of discernment and sensitivity to the Holy Spirit.

V. THE GOLDEN ANOINTING

A. My Personal Encounter with Jesus
We each have defining moments in our lives and ministries. An encounter I had with the Lord Jesus Christ right after I graduated from college has forever changed my life.

B. Two Drops of the Golden Anointing
In this visionary encounter, I felt a single drop of golden anointing oil land on my head—one drop. Then another came. I looked up again and saw a pitcher over my head. The Holy Spirit spoke to me and said, *"Today I am giving you two drops of My golden anointing. One is for you and one you are to give to your wife."*

C. A Promise Given
In that defining moment, He promised me that if I would be faithful with the one drop He had given to me, a day would come when I would receive more of the golden anointing. *"As you are faithful with this, there will be a day I will pour the golden anointing upon your head."* I still live for the fullness of that day.

VI. THERE IS A HIGHER REALM

A. Ministry Proceeds on Three Different Levels
1. By Faith
2. By the Gifts of the Holy Spirit
3. The Glory Realm of God

B. There Is Always Another Realm
Have you plateaued in your walk with Him? Do you hunger for another dimension? Rest assured, there is always more of God to experience and encounter! Yes, just for you!

C. When All Things Are Possible
By faith all things are possible. Greater works are available for every true believer in Christ Jesus to step into. So let's go on a journey together where all things are possible.

VII. JOIN ME IN SURRENDERING YOUR SENSES

A. I Surrender All – All to Jesus I Surrender
Most of you know that I love the old hymns and that singing seems to unlock my heart. One of those traditional hymns is "I Surrender All."[1] Isn't He worth everything? Have you surrendered everything to Jesus? Yes, Lord, I surrender my whole self to You, including my senses. I long to know You better.

B. An Invitation to an Adventure in the Supernatural Ways of God
Yes, our good, good Father is extending an invitation to each of us to learn from Him and to grow into the next level, another realm. It just requires a willing heart which hungers for more of the Lord Himself.

C. Let's Pray Together!
Father, in Jesus' great name, we present our entire beings to You as an act of obedience and worship. We surrender our five natural senses to you now: our sight, hearing, smell, taste, and touch. Holy Spirit, release Your life giving presence upon us in a fresh manner. We need Your touch upon our lives! We desire an increase in the anointing of God to flow in a higher level in the gifts of the Holy Spirit! Here we are Lord; all that we are and all that we hope to be. We surrender our senses as instruments of righteousness for Jesus Christ sake. Amen and Amen!

Reflection Questions
Lesson One: Surrendering Your Senses to the Holy Spirit

Answers to these questions can be found in the back of the study guide.

Fill in the Blank

1. We have both _____ and _____ senses.

2. Part of the purpose of the gift of _____ is to know_____ from _____.

3. As our discernment increases we must become more in tune with _____.

Multiple Choice — Choose the best answer from the list below:

    A. Discern   C. Surrender

    B. Seeing   D. Practice

4. We must _____ to become adept at seeing in the spirit.

5. We must _____ to interpret correctly what God is communicating.

Continued on the next page.

True or False

6. Discernment is a Gift. You either have it or you don't. _____

7. Surrendering control of our senses to the Holy Spirit is mandatory to accurately discern. _____

8. Practicing Discernment will help us become sensitive to Holy Spirit. _____

Scripture Memorization

9. Write out and memorize Romans 12:1-2.

10. In your opinion why is distinguishing of spirits or discernment important in the body of Christ?

Lesson Two:
Seeing: You Have More than One Set of Eyes

I. **WHEN YOUR EYES BECOME OPENED**

   A. **Ephesians 1:18-19a – Theme Scripture**
   "I pray that the eyes of your heart may be enlightened, so that you will know what is the hope of His calling, what are the riches of the glory of His inheritance in the saints, and what is the surpassing greatness of His power toward us who believe."

   B. **My Personal Experience: Praying to See in the Spirit**
   For a stretch of ten years, I used to pray this scripture prayer daily for myself, figuring that if such a commendable apostolic church as the Ephesians needed that prayer, I needed it much more. I would lay hands upon my own heart and call forth an increase of revelation to flood my inner being. I still pray from these scriptures every week, and I commend you to do the same.

   C. **The Importance of Instruction, Association and Spiritual Culture**
   Some things are not just taught but they are caught. Our spiritual insight and revelatory dimensions will increase as we receive teaching, are a part of a prophetic community, and participate in a supernatural culture.

   D. **Impacted by the Life and Ministry of Bob Jones**
   For years, I prayed that the Lord would allow me to be part of the School of the Prophets, before such a thing existed. After ten years of praying this from my heart, I met the prophetic seer papa, Bob Jones. Though I never attended an official School of the Prophets, I became associated with a revelatory community of strongly gifted leaders who later became known as the "Kansas City Prophets."

II. **TWO PROPHETIC STREAMS: THE SEER AND THE PROPHET**

   A. **Two Distinct Hebrew Words: Nabiy and Chozeh**
   The two Hebrew words *nabiy'* and *chozeh* mean a prophet and a seer. A prophet (nabiy') is, for the most part, an inspired hearer and speaker, while a seer (chozeh) is someone whose inspiration is primarily visual. Seers receive revelation from God but communicate it by describing pictures while prophets speak more by inspiration.

The Discerner Study Guide
Lesson Two: Seeing: You Have More than One Set of Eyes

- B. **Scripture References on the Prophet**
    1. Deuteronomy 18:18 – My words will be in your mouth
    2. Exodus 7:1 – Aaron shall be your prophet
    3. Exodus 4:15-16 – Moses and Aaron's relationship
    4. Jeremiah 1:5, 9 – I ordained you as a prophet

- C. **Scripture References on the Seer**
    1. I Samuel 9:9 – The prophet today used to be called a Seer
    2. II Chronicles 29:30 – They sang the prophetic words of Asaph
    3. II Samuel 24:11 – Gad was David's Seer
    4. II Samuel 7:2 – Nathan was a prophet to the king

III. LESSONS FROM HABAKKUK

- A. **Habakkuk 2:1-3**

    "I will stand on my guard post and station myself on the rampart; and I will keep watch to see what He will speak to me, and how I may reply when I am reproved. Then the Lord answered me and said, 'Record the vision and inscribe it on tablets, that the one who reads it may run. For the vision is yet for the appointed time; it hastens toward the goal and it will not fail. Though it tarries, wait for it; for it will certainly come, it will not delay.'"

- B. **Notice the Importance of the Terms Used**

    "I will keep watch to see what He will speak to me."

    In some way Rhema is couched in vision. Habakkuk 1:1 says, *"...the burden which Habakkuk the prophet saw."* He dedicated himself to *"watch to see"* what the Lord would speak. As we have seen, focusing the eyes of our hearts upon God causes us to become inwardly still, it raises our level of faith and expectancy, and it makes us more fully open to receive from God.

- C. **The Importance of Recording the Vision**
    1. When journaling, find your quality time (if possible) and use it. Avoid times when you are sleepy, fatigued, or anxious.
    2. A simple notebook is fine. Even a recorder can be good.
    3. This is a personal journal—grammar, neatness, and spelling are not critical issues.
    4. Date all entries.
    5. Include dreams, visions, interpretations, personal feelings, and emotions as well.
    6. Expect God's love to be affirmed towards you and then, as you receive it, expect the gifts of the Holy Spirit to be in operation.

7. Rhema is tested against Logos. Have a good knowledge of the Bible so that the Holy Spirit can draw upon that knowledge as you record your experiences.

IV. LESSONS FROM ELISHA IN II KINGS 6

A. II Kings 6:15-17
"Now when the attendant of the man of God had risen early and gone out, behold, an army with horses and chariots was circling the city. And his servant said to him, 'Alas, my master! What shall we do?' So he answered, 'Do not fear, for those who are with us are more than those who are with them.' Then Elisha prayed and said, 'O Lord, I pray, open his eyes that he may see.' And the Lord opened the servant's eyes and he saw; and behold, the mountain was full of horses and chariots of fire all around Elisha."

B. The Following Lessons Are Important to Note
1. One might see while others around him or her do not.
2. One who sees can pray for one who cannot see, and the one who could not see may now see.
3. The one who now sees will be astonished when they do see.
4. The prayer of impartation is not complicated. It is simple as its dependency is upon the relationship with the Holy Spirit.
5. The result will be greater faith and confidence in God.

C. Create a Culture of Faith, Not Fear
There are many distinct ingredients needed for the supernatural activity of the Holy Spirit to flourish. The primary distinction is creating an atmosphere safety to risk in faith, versus fear. Fear paralyzes people with the goal of perfection, while faith propels people forward with the goal of growing.

V. PRESENTS IN THE NIGHT SEASON

A. A Testimony – Five Nights of Spiritual Visions
Years ago, in my beginning stages of growth, for five nights in a row the Holy Spirit woke me up at 2:00 in the morning. I would get out of bed, go into our living room and sit down. Then I would "see" a present come floating down out of heaven into my lap. Every night the present was wrapped in a different color of paper and a different color of ribbon. Then on the fifth night (remembering that the number five represents "grace" in biblical numerology), I remember opening the present that had been given to me.

B. The Last Night – A Distinct Present: A Pair of Eyes
I reached down inside the box on the fifth night and took hold of two objects. They were two glass eyes. I took one in each hand and symbolically placed them over my natural eyes. At that point in time, I had already been seeing in the Spirit to some extent. But after that night, I began to see clearer than I ever had before.

C. Promise Given
After this experience, I started seeing both good and evil. I started seeing both future outpourings of the Spirit and upcoming calamities. I was told, "Now you will see things to come."

VI. SEEING GOOD AND EVIL

A. Discerning Different Classes of Spirits
With the gift of discerning of Spirits we can distinguish different classes of Spirits:
1. Angels of God – both good ones and fallen ones
2. Holy Spirit – in various manifestations and movements
3. Human Spirit – knowing the motivation of the heart
4. Demonic Spirits – names, characteristics, activities, etc.

B. Seeing Good
One of the greatest revelations granted to the body of Christ in recent years is an understanding of the "goodness of God." We really do have a good, good Father! The more we comprehend this truth, the more we will grasp seeing what is good. We will know the holy from the profane.

C. Seeing Evil
At the same time, an increase in discerning of spirits concerning evil or demonic activity is also occurring. We must also grow in this area to be able to set the captives free.

D. The Reponses Needed
Every invitation into "seeing in the spirit realm" is a call into divine cooperation. One of the major keys is worshipping the Lord. Positioning yourself before God in humble worship can be one of the best enhancements to growth in the visionary or seer realm.

VII. JOIN ME IN SURRENDERING YOUR EYES

A. Open the Eyes of My Heart Lord

"Open the Eyes of my Heart"[2] is a well-known contemporary Christian song that expresses the deep desire for an increase in the work of the Holy Spirit. This song is a prayer based on theme Scripture for this lesson, Ephesians 1:17-19.

B. An Invitation to See in the Spirit

The scepter of King Jesus has been lowered and He is inviting us to come before Him, minister to Him, and receive more from Him. He simply says, "Come!"

C. Let's Pray Together!

Father, in Jesus' mighty name, once again we present our entire beings to You. We pray according to your Word that you would enlighten the eyes of our hearts with an increase of the spirit of wisdom and revelation, so that we can see what You see. We want to be more effective for Your purposes. We surrender our physical and spiritual eyes to you and ask for an increase of your gifting and anointing to rest upon our eyes. By the grace of God, we believe that we are receiving an increase of visions, dreams and encounters for the glory of God. Amen and Amen.

Reflection Questions
Lesson Two: Seeing: You Have More than One Set of Eyes

Answers to these questions can be found in the back of the study guide.

Fill in the Blank

1. We need the gift of discernment to properly differentiate the _____ from the _____.

2. Seeing in the spirit can include both _____ and _____.

3. We should _____ our spiritual experiences for accuracy and clearer understanding of what the Holy Spirit is communicating.

Multiple Choice — Choose the best answer from the list below:

    A. Rhema   C. Chozeh
    B. Logos   D. Nabiy

4. _____ is generally known as the spoken word of God.

5. The Hebrew word describing one who primarily sees visions or pictures from God is _____.

Continued on the next page.

True or False

6. Seeing and hearing in the spirit realm are related. _____

7. When we see in the spirit realm, we see only good things. _____

8. Seeing in the spirit is like seeing in the natural and needs little or no interpretation. _____

Scripture Memorization

9. Write out and memorize Ephesians 1:18-19

10. Why is it important to sense the spiritual realm?

Lesson Three:
Hearing: Whatever He Hears, He Will Speak

I. WHEN THE SPIRIT OF TRUTH SPEAKS

A. John 16:13 – Theme Scripture
"But when He, the Spirit of truth, comes, He will guide you into all the truth; for He will not speak on His own initiative, but whatever He hears, He will speak; and He will disclose to you what is to come."

B. He Guides You into Truth
1. The Spirit of Truth Has Come
2. He Will Guide You
3. He Listens and Then Speaks
4. He Discloses

C. My Personal Beginnings
My journey of growing up in rural Missouri included many long walks with many long talks. I developed a conversational relationship with God as a youth. Over the years, I have attempted to maintain this style of intimate communion with God and I commend it to you as well. Pour your heart out to Him; then stop and listen to His reply.

D. Lessons Along the Way
We each have significant lessons that alter the course of our lives. For me, one of these was when the Holy Spirit spoke directly to my heart and stated, "Your life is not your own. It belongs to another." This lesson has stuck with me all my days. Always remember, you were bought with a price. You are not your own!

II. GOD STILL SPEAKS

A. Deuteronomy 8:3 – Old Testament Revelation
"He humbled you and let you be hungry, and fed you with manna which you did not know, nor did your fathers know, that He might make you understand that man does not live by bread alone, but man lives by everything that proceeds out of the mouth of the Lord."

B. 4 Key Components
1. Humility
2. Hunger
3. Being Fed
4. Understanding

C. Matthew 4:4 – New Testament Confirmation

"But He [Jesus] answered and said, 'It is written, "Man shall not live by bread alone, but on every word that proceeds out of the mouth of God."'"

III. IT TAKES TWO TO COMMUNICATE

A. Lessons from John 10:27
"My sheep hear my voice, I know them and they follow me."

B. Lessons from Revelation 3:20
"Behold, I stand at the door and I knock; if anyone hears My voice and opens the door, I will come in to him and will dine with him, and he with Me."

C. These Verses Depict Interaction
1. There is initiation and there is response.
2. How does communication actually work?
3. Who initiates? Who responds? Who Listens?
4. Answer: The voice of those in love.
5. We each have a distinct part to play.
6. Make sure your interaction is not just problem-oriented.
7. God shares secrets with His friends.
8. Are you a trusted friend or only a messenger?

IV. EXPECTING TO HEAR GOD'S MANY EXPRESSIONS

A. Lessons from Isaiah 50:4-5
"The Lord God has given Me the tongue of disciples, that I may know how to sustain the weary one with a word. He awakens Me morning by morning, He awakens My ear to listen as a disciple. The Lord has opened My ear; and I was not disobedient nor did I turn back."

B. Lessons from Hebrews 3:13, 15b
"But encourage one another day after day, as long as it is still called 'Today,' so that none of you will be hardened by the deceitfulness of sin."

"Today if you hear His voice, do not harden your hearts, as when they provoked Me."

C. Lessons from Revelation 1:10, 15b

"I was in the Spirit on the Lord's Day, and I heard behind me a loud voice like the sound of a trumpet."

"His voice was like the sound of many rushing waters."

D. The Diversity of God's Voice
1. Impressions
2. Inner audible voice
3. External audible voice
4. Other audible sounds
5. The audible voice of angels
6. Dream language
7. Visions and their many expressions
8. Sounds of heaven on earth

V. HEARING GOOD AND EVIL

A. God's Voice versus the Evil Voice
The Following 8 Points Are Important to Note:
1. God Leads You – Evil Pushes You
2. God Stills You – Evil Rushes You
3. God Reassures You – Evil Frightens You
4. God Enlightens You – Evil Confuses You
5. God Encourages You – Evil Discourages You
6. God Comforts You – Evil Worries You
7. God Calms You – Evil Causes Obsession
8. God Gives You Conviction – Evil Condemns You

B. The Necessity of Learning the Methods and Motivations of Each Realm
We need to learn more than just the proper mechanics of receiving spiritual revelation to grow in hearing God's voice. We must cooperate with the inner workings of the Holy Spirit to bring our heart motivations into progressive cleansing.

C. Testing What You Hear
1. By the Word of God
2. By the Character of God
3. By the Witness of the Holy Spirit
4. By the Fruit It Bears

VI. IMPACTED BY THE LIFE OF MAHESH CHAVDA

A. Mahesh's Personal Background
Mahesh Chavda grew up in Kenya, Africa into a Hindu family of Indian descent. He converted to faith in the Lord Jesus Christ and then came to the United States to receive an education. Mahesh would go on two forty days fasts every year and seek the Lord with prayer. He has moved in all the gifts of the Holy Spirit and has a rich testimony of seeing healings, miracles, and souls being saved. Mahesh has been a forerunner as a Healing Evangelist in this generation and I have been honored to walk with him for many years.

B. My Question: How Do You Hear the Voice of God?
Have you ever asked a teacher a question and ended up with an answer you did not expect? I recall the time I asked my friend and mentor, Mahesh Chavda, how he heard the voice of the Holy Spirit so well. His response marked me, "Oh you must understand, the closer I get to Him the quieter His voice becomes."

C. Personal Determination
I want to be one who will lean into God. I want to be a modern-day John, the beloved, who leans my head upon the chest of my Messiah. Don't you?

VII. JOIN ME IN SURRENDERING YOUR HEARING

A. I Come to the Garden Alone[3]
This hymn has meant more in my life than any other. "And the voice I hear following on my ear, the Son of God discloses. And He walks with me and He talks with me." Can it get any better?

B. An Invitation to Hear in the Spirit
The Holy Spirit wants you to hear His voice more than you want to hear it. We think we are waiting on Him, but could it be that He is waiting on us to simply come and be with Him for a while?

C. Let's Pray Together!

Gracious Father, in Jesus' wonderful name, we present our physical and spiritual ears to You. We want to be modern-day disciples like John the beloved, leaning our heads upon Your chest to hear Your very heartbeat. According to your Word, we ask that You open our ears every morning to hear Your life-giving words. We want to hear Your inspiring and convicting voice both for our sakes and for the sake of others. We want to be more effective for Your purposes. So, we surrender our physical and spiritual ears to you and ask for an increase of your gifting and anointing to rest upon our ears. By the grace of God, we believe that we are receiving an increase of Your voice in our lives for the glory of God. Amen and Amen.

Reflection Questions
Lesson Three: Hearing: Whatever He Hears, He Will Speak

Answers to these questions can be found in the back of the study guide.

Fill in the Blank

1. To hear clearly, we must have our hearts _____.

2. We learn to hear God through time spent _____ and waiting in prayer.

3. Being a _____ of God is more than getting messages and words from Him.

Multiple Choice — Choose the best answer from the list below:

    A.   listen   C.   obey it

    B.   hear   D.   test it

4. When we hear a word from God, we should _____.

5. As we grow closer to God, we can _____ His voice more clearly.

True or False

6. God speaks in many different ways. _____

7. God's Word will push us closer to Him. _____

8. We should trust that what we hear is from the Holy Spirit. _____

Continued on the next page.

Scripture Memorization

9. Write out John 16:13 and memorize it.

10. What can you change in your life to hear the voice of God more clearly?

Lesson Four:
Feeling: From the Heart Flows the Issues of Life

I. **WATCHING OVER YOUR HEART**

    A. **Proverbs 4:23 – Theme Scripture**
"Watch over your heart with all diligence, for from it flows the springs of life."

    B. **Review of the Five Senses – Natural and Supernatural**
1. Eyes: Sight – Seeing Visions and Having Dreams
2. Ears: Hearing – Voices and Sounds
3. Heart: Touch – Feelings and Emotions
4. Tongue: Taste – Both Good and Bad
5. Nose: Smell – Fragrances and Aromas

    C. **Foundational Understanding Is Needed**
1. Sin Hardens the Heart – Hebrews 3:13
2. Love Not the World – I John 2:15
3. God's Word Is a Hammer – Jeremiah 23:29
4. Fix Your Hope on Him – I John 3:3
5. The Blood of Jesus Christ Cleanses Us from All Unrighteousness – II Corinthians 7:1, I John 1:9

    D. **My Personal Approach**
1. I Pray Over the Condition of My Own Heart
2. I Am Accepted in the Beloved
3. I Choose Being Sensitive vs. Being Reactive

II. **THE EMOTIONS OF GOD AND MAN**

    A. **Mark 5:25-34 – The Woman with the Issue of Blood**
"If only I can touch His clothes, I shall be made well."
"And Jesus knowing that power (virtue) had gone out of Him…"
"Who touched my clothes?"
"His disciples said to Him, 'Who touched my clothes?'"
"Daughter, your faith has made you well."

    B. **Jesus Was Moved with Compassion**
1. Matthew 9:6 – *and seeing the multitudes…*
2. Mark 1:41 – *Jesus stretched out His Hand and touched him…*
3. Matthew 15:32 – *I feel compassion for the people…*
4. Luke 7:13 – *When He saw her…*
5. Luke 15:20 – *his father saw him and felt compassion for him…*

C. Insight from the Generals of the Faith
1. "You must learn to love the sick." - Testimony of Oral Roberts
2. *"Only Love Can Make a Miracle"* - Testimony of Mahesh Chavda
3. "You must learn to stop for the one." - Testimony of Heidi Baker
4. "Everything God does is related to Who He is." - Testimony of John Wimber

III. GOD'S HEART IN MAN'S HEART

A. It's the Heart that Matters
1. Jesus came from the bosom (heart) of the Father – John 1:8
2. Jesus resides in our hearts by faith – Colossians 1:26-27
3. We are a temple of the Holy Spirit – I Corinthians 3:16

B. Lessons from John the Beloved
"Peter, turning around, saw the disciple whom Jesus loved following them; the one who also had leaned back on His bosom at the supper and said, 'Lord, who is the one who betrays You?'" John 21:20

John the beloved leaned in and placed His head upon the chest of the Messiah. We can do the same and thus hear his heart and feel His emotions.

C. A Luke 24 Experience – Road to Emmaus Awaits Us All
1. There is initiation and there is response.
2. Does your heart burn warmly within?
3. What is your relationship with the Written Word of God?
4. There is an encounter waiting just for you with the Word of God and the God of the Word!

IV. LESSONS IN BURDEN BEARING

A. Lessons from Galatians 6:2
"Bear one another's burdens and thus fulfill the law of Christ."

B. Lessons in Prophetic Intercession
1. It is necessary to discern atmospheres
2. What is the origin of what you are feeling?
3. Is it yours, someone else's, etc.?
4. Is it demonic or the flesh?
5. Avoid being judgmental and critical
6. Remember the fruit of the Spirit
7. God always has a solution

C. **Lessons from Jesus – Journey into Jerusalem**
Jesus was carried into His divine assignment in Jerusalem on the back of a young colt or donkey. If God can use a donkey, He can use me!

D. **Carry the Cargo and Release It to the Throne of God**
There are many wisdom lessons to learn in the art of prophetic intercession or burden bearing in prayer. Too often intercessors—or people of prayer—carry the burden of the Lord too long or in a wrong way, thus they become weighed down, depressed and weary. We are to pick up the cares and distresses of others but then offload them at the throne of grace. Take them and release them to throne of the Almighty God!

V. **FEELING THE SENSATION OF GOOD AND EVIL**

A. **We Walk by Faith – II Corinthians 5:7**
"For we walk by faith and not by sight."

B. **Renewing of our Mind – Romans 12:1-2**
"Therefore I urge you, brethren, by the mercies of God, to present your bodies a living and holy sacrifice, acceptable to God, which is your spiritual service of worship. And do not be conformed to this world, but be transformed by the renewing of your mind, so that you may prove what the will of God is, that which is good and acceptable and perfect."

C. **Annoyed in the Spirit – Acts 16:16-18**
"It happened that as we were going to the place of prayer a slave-girl having a spirit of divination met us who was bringing her masters much profit by fortune telling. Following after Paul and us, she kept crying out, saying, 'These men are bond-servants of the Most High God, who are proclaiming to you the way of salvation.' She continued doing this for many days. But Paul was greatly annoyed, and turned and said to the spirit, 'I command you in the name of Jesus Christ to come out of her!' And it came out at that very moment."

D. **Testing the Motivational Spirit Behind a Manifestation**
1. By the Word of God
2. By the Character of God
3. By the Witness of the Holy Spirit
4. By the Gifts of the Holy Spirit
5. By the Fruit It Bears over Time

VI. IMPACTED BY THE LIFE OF CINDY JACOBS

A. Cindy's Personal Background – Generals of Intercession
Cindy Jacobs, another dear friend and comrade of mine, has travelled the world teaching believers how to hear the voice of God and to respond to the burden of the Lord in prayer. She has ministered to numerous world leaders while at the same time, carrying a heart of compassion for the needs of the everyday person. Cindy is known for her strong prophetic anointing and keen operation in the gifts of the Holy Spirit.

B. I Was in the Spirit – Revelation 1:9-10
The phrase *"egennomehn ehn pneumati"* literally means "to become in the Spirit," a state in which one could see visions and be informed or spoken to directly by the Spirit of God. Therein lies the secret to receiving revelation—worship the Lord and be led by (or walk in) the Spirit!

C. Something Just Shifted!
Operating in the combination of "hearing, seeing and feeling," I have been with Cindy Jacobs in multiple cities and nations and have heard her say things such as, "Something just shifted! Did you feel that?" Yes, you can shift atmospheres in Jesus' great name.

VII. JOIN ME IN SURRENDERING YOUR HEART – YOUR SENSE OF TOUCH

A. He Touched Me – Oh He Touched Me![4]
One of the all-time great Gospel songs inspirationally declares, "He touched me. Oh He touched me." This is what believing believer's need today! We need to experience a fresh touch from God ourselves. The Good News is that He is ready to give strength to the weary in any situation and for every circumstance.

B. An Invitation to Sense the Heart of God
Do you want to Sense the Heart of God? Do you want to feel what the Holy Spirit is feeling? Do you want to grow your heart to overflow with the life of God?

C. Let's Pray Together!

Father, in Jesus' great name, we present our minds, our wills and our emotions to You. We choose to watch over our hearts so that a river of life will come out of us to impact others. Send forth your word to shatter any stony places remaining in our hearts. We surrender our physical and spiritual hearts to You and ask for an increase of Your gifting and anointing to rest upon our sensitivity and emotions. By the grace of God, we believe that we are receiving an increase of Your feelings, emotions and compassion in our lives for the glory of God. Amen and Amen.

Reflection Questions
Lesson Four: Feeling: From the Heart Flows the Issues of Life

Answers to these questions can be found in the back of the study guide.

Fill in the Blank

1. As our minds are renewed, we can more accurately prove the will of _____.

2. One key to receiving revelation is to _____ the Lord and be led by the Holy Spirit!

3. Feeling God's _____ toward a certain situation will help us understand the true motivations behind it.

Multiple Choice — Choose the best answer from the list below:

    A. burden   C. identity

    B. word   D. works

4. Sometimes, God wants us to release the _____ He gave us back to Him.

5. God's deeds are an expression of His _____.

True or False

6. Discernment of the heart can take many forms. ____

7. All true words come from God. ____

8. We can feel God's emotions. ____

Continued on the next page.

Scripture Memorization

9. Write out Romans 12:1-2 and memorize it.

10. What impressed you most from this lesson on feeling the heart of God?

Lesson Five:
Tasting, Smelling & Other Leadings

I. OUR SENSES BECOME HEIGHTENED

A. Psalm 119:103 and II Corinthians 2:14 – Theme Scriptures

"How sweet are Your words to my taste! Yes, sweeter than honey to my mouth!" Psalm 119:103 NASB

"Now thanks be to God, who always leads us as captives in Christ's triumphal procession and uses us to spread the aroma of the knowledge of him everywhere." II Corinthians 2:14 NIV

B. When One Sense Is Lost
1. How do we respond when there is the loss of one sense?
2. The loss of one sense can be turned to gain as other senses may become heightened.
3. The life of Helen Keller gives wisdom and understanding, and demonstrates this principle. Consider the life of Helen Keller who was deaf, blind and mute. But through perseverance, she learned to use her other senses and become an influential leader despite her many hindrances.

C. Radio Analogy – Stuck on One Channel
1. There are different times and seasons
2. God's WWW: Will, Word and His Ways
3. Be flexible and yielding
4. Identify the hindrances
5. Cultivate the hunger
6. Be patient; it will all work together for good

D. Impact from the Life and Ministry of Patricia King
Patricia King of XP Ministries and XP Media is an amazing pioneer and entrepreneur in the church world, in media, justice, business and other realms. She is always learning, always child-like, always believing and trusting the Lord, and eager to learn new ways and new life skills.

II. ADDITIONAL SCRIPTURES REGARDING OUR SENSE OF TASTE

A. Psalm 34:8 – The Goodness of God
"O taste and see that the Lord is Good." NASB

B. Job 6:30 – Discerning Perverse Things
"Is there iniquity in my tongue? Cannot my taste discern perverse things?" KJV

C. Song of Songs 2:3 – Discerning the Lord's Presence
"As the apple tree among the trees of the wood, so is my beloved among the songs. I sat down under his shadow with great delight, and his fruit was sweet to my taste." KJV

D. Jeremiah 1:9 – Example of Combination Anointing
"Then the Lord stretched out His hand and touched my mouth, and the Lord said to me, "Behold, I have put My words in your mouth." NASB

III. PASSING THE TASTE TEST

A. Cooking Competition
1. The primary concern when judging a cooking competition is: "How does it taste?"
2. The second consideration is the presentation: "How does it look?"
3. Not only do you consider how it tastes, but also how it compares to other tastes?

B. Fruit Tastes Good!
1. As it is in the natural, so it is in the spiritual—fruit tastes good! The fruit of the Spirit—love, joy, peace, patience, kindness, goodness, faithfulness, gentleness, and self-control (Galatians 5:22)—is a delight to our eyes and to our taste.
2. The Word of God tastes good to our mouth and stomach (Ezekiel 3:1-3).

C. When Something Leaves a Bad Taste in Your Mouth
1. There is something rotten going on here.
2. What is the source of the "bad taste?" Perhaps it shows that something needs to be healed in your life or someone else's, a generational issue, a territorial issue, etc.

IV. ADDITIONAL SCRIPTURES ON OUR SENSE OF SMELL

A. Genesis 8:20-21 – The Power of Inhaling and Exhaling
"Then Noah built an altar to the Lord, and took of every clean animal and of every clean bird and offered burnt offerings on the altar. The Lord smelled the soothing aroma; and the Lord said to Himself, "I will never again curse the ground on account of man, for the intent of man's

heart is evil from his youth; and I will never again destroy every living thing, as I have done." NASB

B. Philippians 4:18 – An Acceptable Sacrifice
"But I have received everything in full and have an abundance; I am amply supplied, having received from Epaphroditus what you have sent, a fragrant of aroma, an acceptable sacrifice, well-pleasing to God." NASB

C. Song of Songs 4:11 – The Aroma of His Love
"Your lips, my bride, drip honey; honey and milk are under your tongue, and the fragrance of your garments is like the fragrance of Lebanon." NASB

D. Leviticus 1:9 – The Offering Made by Fire
"And the priest shall burn all on the altar as a burnt sacrifice, an offering made by fire, a sweet aroma to the Lord." NKJV

V. SNIFFING OUT GOOD AND EVIL

A. Good Versus Evil
Important Points to Keep in Focus:
1. Good Exalts God – Evil Exalts a Person
2. Good Endures the Test of Time – Evil Rushes You to Come to Quick Conclusions
3. Good Aligns with the Word of God – Evil Paints Outside the Lines
4. Good Promotes Purity – Evil Allures you to Perversity
5. Good Promotes Solid Doctrine – Evil Promotes Twisted Belief Systems
6. Good Values Community – Evil Promotes Isolationism
7. Good Values Humility – Evil Results in Elitism

B. "Something Doesn't Smell Right Here!"
Have you heard this saying before? You must learn to trust your senses to discern good and evil. Often if something doesn't smell or seem right, it isn't.

C. "This Just Tastes Right!"
Here is another common statement that can be loaded with discernment. You can taste and see that the Lord is good. It just tastes right!

D. **Testing What You Sense**
1. You rely on prayer.
2. You rely on your ability to hear answers from the Holy Spirit (combined with the other things in this list).
3. You rely on the internal witness of the Holy Spirit.
4. You rely on the principles of the Word of God.
5. You rely on the agreement of others.
6. You rely on your previous experience.
7. You rely on the fruit it bears.

VI. ACTIVATING OUR SENSES

A. **Examples from the Life and Ministry of Jerame Nelson**
I have the blessing of walking with many leaders in the body of Christ, both peers as well as next generation leaders. Jerame Nelson of Elisha Revolution is a great example of someone who knows the culture of honor, walks with others, and yet does not let his high-level gifting intimidate others. Instead, I have witnessed how Jerame learns from others, even in areas of discernment, and yet expands upon them through his own calling, faith and experiences.

B. **An Observation and a Pondering**
What can I still learn? Am I too old to learn new understandings and expressions? Are you hungry enough to break out of the box of limitations or cessationism and cry out to the Lord for more?

C. **Personal Determination – Provoked to Godly Jealousy**
How am I going to personally respond to the questions above? I intend to be aligned with the Joining of the Generations. I want to see the synergy of three generations walking together in a generation so that there will be a sustained move of the Holy Spirit.

VII. JOIN ME IN SURRENDERING ALL YOUR SENSES

A. **Tis So Sweet to Trust in Jesus!**[5]
This trustworthy old hymn teaches us a basic truth to help us continue to move forward in God. "Tis so sweet to trust in Jesus and to take Him at His Word." All I can add is, "Yes and Amen!"

B. **An Invitation to Taste and Smell in the Spirit**
Once again, even in the areas you might be less exposed to, I challenge you to be hungry and learn new dimensions in the Holy Spirit.

C. Let's Pray Together!

Heavenly Father, in Jesus' great name, we present our senses of taste and smell to You. According to your Word, we ask that You would anoint these members of our bodies to be used under the power and gifts of the Holy Spirit to discern good and evil. By the grace of God, we believe that we are receiving an increase of Your revelatory and wisdom ways in our lives for the purposes of God. Praise the Lord! Amen and Amen.

Reflection Questions
Lesson Five: Tasting, Smelling & Other Leadings

Answers to these questions can be found in the back of the study guide.

Fill in the Blank

1. Our spiritual taste and smell help us determine the _____ source of a situation.

2. We must combine other elements of discernment with taste and smell to determine God's _____ in a situation.

Multiple Choice — Choose the best answer from the list below:

    A.   smell   C.   sweet

    B.   sound   D.   savory

3. In Leviticus, God describes sacrifices as having a _____ aroma.

4. When a situation looks right on the surface, but your discernment is not in agreement, you could say, "This just doesn't _____ right.

Continued on the next page.

True or False

5. We should act quickly when our spiritual taste or smell is activated. _____

6. The Bible uses "sweet aroma" as an illustration of how God views offerings given in the right spirit. _____

7. We should rely on our spiritual taste and smell as the final authority for truth. _____

Scripture Memorization

8. Write out Galatians 5:22 and memorize it.

9. In what areas of your life do you see the importance of the spiritual senses of taste and smell? Why?

Lesson Six:
Knowing: The Sixth Sense

I. **KNOWING AS A SPIRITUAL SENSE**

   A. **I Corinthians 2:16 – Theme Scripture**
   "For WHO HAS KNOWN THE MIND OF THE LORD, THAT HE WILL INSTRUCT HIM? But we have the mind of Christ."

   B. **Review of the 5 Senses – Plus One**
   1. Eyes: Seeing – Visions and Dreams
   2. Ears: Hearing – Voices and Sounds
   3. Heart: Feeling – Feelings and Emotions
   4. Tongue: Tasting – Both Good and Bad
   5. Nose: Smelling – Fragrances and Aromas
   6. Mind: Knowing – Thoughts and Impressions

   C. **Behind the Scenes I Have Wondered**
   Is this "déjà vu?" What is this? How do I know this? Have I seen this before? Why have I seen this before? Is what I am sensing actual or visual only? There are many questions that can be asked, but the primary one that must be discerned is, "What is the source of the experience?"

   D. **Lessons Along the Way**
   Often, when I have seen something or known something before I experience it, I am aware of one major issue. "I am in the right place at the right time." The Lord can use these kinds of leadings or knowings as tools of letting you know you are right on track!

II. **KEY SCRIPTURES ON KNOWING**

   A. **Isaiah 55:8-11 – The Nature of God's Thoughts**
   "'For My thoughts are not your thoughts, nor are your ways My ways,' declares the LORD. 'For as the heavens are higher than the earth, so are My ways higher than your ways and My thoughts than your thoughts. For as the rain and the snow come down from heaven, and do not return there without watering the earth and making it bear and sprout, and furnishing seed to the sower and bread to the eater; so will My word be which goes forth from My mouth; It will not return to Me empty, without accomplishing what I desire, and without succeeding in the matter for which I sent it.'"

B. I Chronicles 12:31 – Sons of Issachar
"Of the sons of Issachar, men who understood the times, with knowledge of what Israel should do, their chiefs were two hundred; and all their kinsmen were at their command."

C. Matthew 9:4 – Jesus Knowing Their Hearts
"And Jesus knowing their thoughts said, "Why are you thinking evil in your hearts?"

D. Luke 9:47 – Jesus Knowing Their Thoughts
"But Jesus, knowing what they were thinking in their hearts, took a child and stood him by His side..."

E. John 13:3 – Jesus Knowing the Father
"Jesus, knowing that the Father had given all things into His hands, and that He had come forth from God and was going back to God..."

III. YOU CAN HAVE THE MIND OF CHRIST
When you apply wisdom applications to the following scriptures, you will be walking in a realm of the Mind of Christ.

A. Lessons from James 1:5-8
"But if any of you lacks wisdom, let him ask of God, who gives to all generously and without reproach, and it will be given to him. But he must ask in faith without any doubting, for the one who doubts is like the surf of the sea, driven and tossed by the wind. For that man ought not to expect that he will receive anything from the Lord, being a double-minded man, unstable in all his ways."

B. Lessons from I Corinthians 1:30-31
"But by His doing you are in Christ Jesus, who became to us wisdom from God, and righteousness and sanctification, and redemption, so that, just as it is written, "LET HIM WHO BOASTS, BOAST IN THE LORD."

C. Lessons from James 4:2b
"You do not have because you do not ask."

D. Lessons from I Corinthians 2:16b
"But we have the mind of Christ."

E. Lessons from Mark 11:24
"Therefore I say to you, all things for which you pray and ask, believe that you have received them, and they will be granted you."

IV. KNOWINGS AND THE GIFTS OF THE HOLY SPIRIT

A. The Word of Knowledge
1. What? Details like Names, Dates, Locations, Pains
2. How? Seeing, Hearing, Thoughts, Knowing
3. Can you think of examples of this from your own life?

B. B. The Gift of Prophesy
1. What? Words of Edification, Exhortation, Comfort
2. How? Seeing, Hearing, Flowing, Thoughts, Knowing
3. What are examples of this gift from the lives of others you know?

C. The Gift of Faith
1. What? Portion of God's Faith – Supernatural Surge of Confidence
2. How? Gut Feeling, You Can't Shake It Off!
3. What are some examples in scripture where you know the gift of faith was in operation?

D. The Gift of Discernings of Spirits
1. What? Perceiving the Motivational Spirit behind Manifestations
2. How? Seeing, Hearing, Knowing
3. What are some categories or classifications of the demonic that the gift of discernings of spirits distinguishes or reveals?

V. WALKING IN DIVINE INTELLIGENCE

It is my conviction that there will yet emerge, believers of an excellent spirit who walk in a level of "knowings" that builds on, yet surpasses, the gift of a word of knowledge. In the days toward which we are headed, this new level of revelation will include the understanding of the seven Spirits of God (see Isaiah 11:1-3) and Divine Intelligence (see Daniel 1:17).

A. Inspiration from the Life of Daniel – Daniel 1:17
"As for these four youths, God gave them knowledge and intelligence in every branch of literature and wisdom; Daniel even understood all kinds of visions and dreams."

B. Promises – Daniel 11:32b
"But the people who know their God will display strength and take action."

C. A Look to the Future – Daniel 12:4
"But you, Daniel, shut up the words, and seal the book until the time of the end; many shall run to and fro, and knowledge shall increase."

D. Calling Forth Hope Solutions – I Thessalonians 5:8
"But since we are of the day, let us be sober, having put on the breastplate of faith and love, and as a helmet, the hope of salvation."

VI. OBSERVATIONS FROM THE LIFE OF CHUCK PIERCE

A. Chuck Pierce's Background
One of the strongest Issachar-knowing prophets in the body of Christ today is Chuck Pierce from Glory of Zion International Ministries. The Lord uses Chuck's background in economics and the business world, and blends it together with the prophetic gifts of the Holy Spirit. Chuck is thus often able to discern the prophetic destinies of cities and nations.

B. Issachar Anointing – Knowing the Times and the Seasons
"Of the sons of Issachar, men who understood the times, with the knowledge of what Israel should do, their chiefs were two hundred; and all their kinsman were at their command." 1 Chronicles 12:32

C. Personal Determination
I want to be one who walks in "Divine Intelligence" knowing the "Times and the Seasons" and having "Hope Solutions" for my generation. Therefore, I conclude, that I will not partner with the spirit of fear but rather one of faith.

VII. JOIN ME IN SURRENDERING YOUR MIND TO CHRIST

A. My Hope Is Built on Nothing Less
To be a people who offer "Hope Solutions" with divine knowings, we need to put on the helmet of salvation. We must surrender our thoughts to those of Christ Jesus. In fact, we must have our foundation built on Christ the solid rock. Christ is the answer.

B. An Invitation to Know in the Spirit Realm
The Holy Spirit is offering a higher realm of supernatural knowledge to solve man's dilemmas. The invitation into divine knowledge is being released today.

C. Let's Pray Together!

Heavenly Father, in Jesus' name, we present our minds to you. According to your Word, we have not because we ask not. Therefore, we admit our need, we declare Your vast supply, and we ask for Your divine thoughts and Your divine knowings to be released to each of us. We surrender our physical and spiritual minds to the Holy Spirit and put on the helmet of Hope. By the grace of God, we believe that we are receiving an increase of Your revelation in our hearts and minds for Jesus Christ's sake. Amen and Amen.

Reflection Questions
Lesson Six: Knowing: The Sixth Sense

Answers to these questions can be found in the back of the study guide.

Fill in the Blank

1. Part of knowing is Perceiving the _____ Spirit behind Manifestations.

2. We must not partner with the spirit of fear but rather one of _____.

3. _____ can come to us as a gut feeling, we can't shake off.

Multiple Choice — Choose the best answer from the list below:

    A.   solutions   C.   knowledge

    B.   seeing   D.   ideas

4. One facet of "Knowing" is advance _____ of events,

5. God can give us _____ to issues that we know little or nothing about. This is usually referred to as divine intelligence.

Continued on the next page.

True or False

6. The knowing part of discernment is related to the gift of faith. _____

7. Knowings come to us by seeing and hearing. _____

8. We must discern the source of knowings before we act on them. _____

Scripture Memorization

9. Write out I Corinthians 2:15-16 and memorize it.

10. How has this lesson changed your perspective on how we can interact with God?

Section Two:

Discerning Revelation

Lesson Seven:
Testing the Spirits: Don't Believe Every Spirit!

I. **TEST THE SPIRITS – DO NOT BE NAIVE!**

   A. **I John 4:1 – Theme Scripture**
   "Beloved, do not believe every spirit, but test the spirits to see whether they are from God, because many false prophets have gone out into the world."

   B. **We Must Discern Revelation, Not Just Receive It!**
   1. Do not believe every spirit.
   2. God wants us to "test the spirits."
   3. Be on the alert—false prophets exist.
   4. We have not received a spirit of fear.
   5. Have faith in God to lead us and protect us.

   C. **Key Foundational Points**
   1. Do not become demon-centered.
   2. Be God-centered.
   3. Worshipping God is a major key.
   4. Do not give away to others the power of making your own decisions.
   5. Walk in honor toward those in authority.

   D. **Lessons I Learned Early in My Christian Life**
   1. There is power in the name and blood of Jesus!
   2. There is power is the spoken word of God.
   3. There is power in forgiveness.
   4. The work of the cross of Christ is perfect.
   5. Jesus declared on the cross, *"It is finished!"*

II. **TESTING THE SPIRITS IS BIBLICAL AND NECESSARY**
When the following scriptures are combined, they provide powerful lessons in *"Testing the Spirits."*

   A. **I Thessalonians 5:20-22 – Examine Everything**
   "Do not despise prophetic utterances. But examine everything carefully; hold fast to that which is good; abstain from every form of evil."

B. I John 4:2-3 – Jesus Christ Has Come in the Flesh
"By this you know the Spirit of God: every spirit that confesses that Jesus Christ has come in the flesh is from God; and every spirit that does not confess Jesus is not from God; this is the spirit of the antichrist, of which you have heard that it is coming, and now it is already in the world."

C. Matthew 12:33 – The Tree Is Known by Its Fruit
"Either make the tree good and its fruit good, or make the tree bad and its fruit bad; for the tree is known by its fruit."

D. Revelation 19:10 – Testimony of Jesus
"Then I fell at his feet to worship him. But he said to me, "Do not do that; I am a fellow servant of yours and your brethren who hold the testimony of Jesus; worship God. For the testimony of Jesus is the spirit of prophecy."

III. NINE SCRIPTURAL TESTS OF DIVINE REVELATION

This material is presented in a few of my other Study Guides and Classes. But the content is so valuable I have included a revised edition in this study guide as well.

A. I Corinthians 14:3 – It Must Build the Recipient Up
"But one who prophesies speaks to men for edification and exhortation and consolation."

The purpose of all true prophetic revelation is to build up, to admonish, and to encourage the people of God. Anything that is not directed to this end is not true prophecy. Consider Jeremiah 1:5, 10. His commission is at first negative, but then with a promise. I Corinthians 14:26 sums it up best – *"Let all things be done unto edification."*

B. II Timothy 3:16 – It Honors the Authority of the Word of God
"All scripture is given by inspiration of God."

All true revelation always agrees with the letter and the spirit of scripture. Read II Corinthians 1:17-20. Where the Holy Spirit says yes and amen in scripture, He also says yes and amen in revelation. He does not contradict Himself.

C. John 16:14 – It Must Glorify God
"He shall glorify Me; for He shall take of Mine, and disclose it to you."

All true revelation centers in Jesus Christ; it exalts and glorifies Him. Read Revelation 19:10.

D. Matthew 7:15-16 – Know Them by Their Fruit
"Beware of false prophets who come to you in sheep's clothing, but inwardly are ravenous wolves...you will know them by their fruits."

True revelation produces fruit in character and conduct that agrees with the fruit of the Holy Spirit. Read Ephesians 5:9 and Galatians 5:22-23. The following characteristics are clearly not the fruit of the Holy Spirit: pride, adultery, boastfulness, exaggeration, dishonesty, covetousness, financial irresponsibility, licentiousness, immorality, addictive appetites, broken marriage vows, and broken homes. Any supposed revelation that is responsible for results such as these is from a channel other than the Holy Spirit.

E. Deuteronomy 18:20-22 – Are the Predictions Fulfilled?
Read this passage of scripture first and then review these points.

If a revelation contains a prediction concerning the future, are these predictions fulfilled? If not, with a few exceptions, the revelation is not from God. Exceptions:

1. The will of the person involved.
2. National repentance – example of Nineveh.
3. Messianic predictions (hundreds of years until fulfilled).
4. Note the difference between Old and New Testament prophets.

F. Deuteronomy 13:1-5 – It Must Direct People to Jesus
Read this passage of scripture first and then review these points.
Even though a person may make a prediction concerning the future which is fulfilled, it does not necessarily prove that the person is moving from Holy Spirit inspired revelation. If such a person, by his own ministry, turns others away from obedience to the one true God, then that person is false – even if he or she makes correct predictions concerning the future.

G. Romans 8:15 – It Releases the Spirit of Adoption
"For you have not received a spirit of slavery leading to fear again, but you have received a spirit of adoption as sons by which we cry out, Abba, Father!"

True revelation, given by the Holy Spirit, produces liberty and not bondage. Read also I Corinthians 14:33 and II Timothy 1:7. The Holy Spirit never brings God's people into a condition where they act like slaves, captured by fear and legal compulsion.

H. II Corinthians 3:6 – Does It Produce Life or Death?
"Who also made us adequate as servants of a new covenant, not of the letter, but of the Spirit; for the letter kills, but the Spirit gives life."

True revelation, given by the Holy Spirit, produces life and not a culture of death.

I. I John 2:27 – It Must Value the Anointing
"And as for you, the anointing which you received from Him abides in you, and you have no need for anyone to teach you; but as His anointing teaches you about all things, and is true and is not a lie, and just as it has taught you, you abide in Him."

True revelation, given by the Holy Spirit, is attested to by the Holy Spirit within the believer. The Holy Spirit is "the Spirit of Truth" (John 16:13). He bears witness to that which is true, but He rejects that which is false. This ninth test is the most subjective of them all and must be used in conjunction with the previous eight objective standards.

IV. MODERN-DAY EXAMPLES AND TESTIMONIES

A. Example from Ministry in Sarajevo, Yugoslavia
I was doing ministry with my friend Mahesh Chavda. He would pray for people and sometimes I would follow up with them. I came up to a young man who was lying on the floor—curled up into a ball. It caught my attention that his extremities were becoming cold, to the point that his hands were turning blue. Clearly something unpleasant and demonic was happening. I prayed for more of the Holy Spirit's anointing, power and presence to come upon this man. With authority I spoke to the hindrance that was keeping this man in bondage, directing it to identify itself.

Suddenly, even though this young man did not speak any English, he opened his mouth and said, "Take the book out"—in clear, unaccented English. I did not need a translator to understand the words. I felt led to turn him onto his side to see if there was a book in his pocket, and sure enough, I found one—a copy of Hitler's *Mein Kampf*. I took it out, and his whole body relaxed and the young man appeared to be set free from all torment.

As it turned out, the man was a student from Hungary, and he was studying communism at a university in Sarajevo. Apparently when I took the book out, the demons left him, they flat-out fled. He immediately got saved and even baptized in the Holy Spirit. He could not stop saying, "Your God Jesus! My God Jesus!" in Hungarian. (Interpreted for me into English.) As you can see, receiving discernment in the situation made it possible to get rid of the unknown hindrance to freedom and salvation.

B. Three Aspects of Discernment Are Needed
Testing the spirits is important in all three of the aspects of discernment: revelation, interpretation, and application, although a different sort of spiritual filter needs to be applied to each aspect. The important thing is that you grow in all three areas of your ministry of discernment.

C. Build Your Own Treasure Chest
What is an example of "Testing the Spirits" from your life or the life of someone else you know?

V. THE NEED FOR DISCERNMENT – TO BE "QUICK OF SCENT"
Because the outward appearance of the wolf is disguised under "sheep's clothing," the human eye does not immediately discern the true identity of the wolf. However, there is an animal connected with the protection of sheep which will not be deceived by the "sheep's clothing"—the sheep dog. The reason he is not deceived is that he does not judge by his eyesight, instead using his sense of smell. The wolf may look like a sheep, but he still smells like a wolf. In scripture, this sense of smell, acting independently of the eyesight, sometimes typifies the discernment which comes through the Holy Spirit.

In Isaiah 11:2-3, the prophet, foreseeing the ministry of Jesus as the Messiah (the Anointed One), declares that the Spirit of the Lord shall make him of quick understanding (literally, quick of scent) in the fear of the Lord: and He shall not judge after the sight of His eyes, neither reprove after the hearing of His ears.

Those to whom God commits the care of His sheep must likewise, through the Holy Spirit, be "quick of scent," so that *"they will not judge after the sight of their eyes, neither reprove after the hearing of their ears."* In this way, they will not depend merely on the evidence of their senses or the reasoning of their natural minds, but will quickly detect the false prophets who come among God's people as "wolves in sheep's clothing."

The sheep dog that fails to bark when the wolf approaches has failed in his responsibility to the flock. In Isaiah 56:10, God says concerning Israel's watchmen under the old covenant, they are all dumb dogs, they cannot bark; sleeping, lying down, loving to slumber. These watchmen of Israel failed God and their people. When the spiritual enemies of God's people approached, these men remained silent, and gave no warning to the flock. As a result, God's people became an easy prey to their enemies.

The same thing has happened many times to God's people, even in this generation.

VI. OBSERVATIONS FROM THE LIFE OF DEREK PRINCE

A. Derek Prince's Background – Great British Bible Teacher
This scholarly believer came from a background as a professor of logic in England. After his dramatic conversion to Christ Jesus he became one of the leading teachers in the global charismatic movement. In my formative years, I personally learned more from this man than any other leader in the body of Christ.

B. Pioneer of Deliverance and Breaking Curses
Derek Prince was not only a teacher of the word but also a doer of it. He taught that one-third of Jesus' ministry was devoted to the ministry of deliverance. Derek Prince then became a pioneer in identifying demonic bondages and curses, and setting the captives free. (For more on this subject see the books *How to Expel Demons, Break Curses and Release Blessings*[6] and *From Curse to Blessing*[7] by Derek Prince.)

C. Knowing the "When and Where" to Confront
The timing of a matter can be imperative. The enemy attempts to push and drive, but the Holy Spirit leads and moves. We must learn our authority in Christ and the wisdom principles that make our ministry effective.

D. Personal Wisdom Lessons Observed
Having been in scores of public and private settings with Derek Prince and others, I observed many wisdom lessons on the "How, When, and Where" concerning spiritual warfare.[8]

VII. JOIN ME IN ASKING GOD FOR HEIGHTENED DISCERNMENT

A. I'm No Longer a Slave to Fear – I Am a Child of God![9]
This is one of the greatest contemporary songs that relates to this generation. It inspires believers to stand in the freedom that Christ Jesus has obtained for us.

B. An Invitation to Test the Spirits
In these last days, testing the spirits is a necessity and not an option. Apply your whole heart to learning the lessons of "Testing the Spirits" so that you can determine the source of revelation.

C. Let's Pray Together!
Gracious Father, in Jesus' name, we trust in Your ability to lead us and protect us more than we do the devil's power to deceive us. We declare that we have not received a spirit of fear, but power, love and a sound mind. We choose to honor Your Word by examining everything and holding on to that which is good. We choose to honor those in authority while asking that you sharpen our capacities to grow in discernment from the Holy Spirit. By the grace of God, we believe that we are receiving an increase in our lives to test the spirits to see if they originate from God. Thank You, God, for the increase of light, knowledge and revelation. Amen and Amen.

Reflection Questions
Lesson Seven: Testing the Spirits: Don't Believe Every Spirit!

Answers to these questions can be found in the back of the study guide.

Fill in the Blank

1. We must _____ the spirit behind everything we hear from the spirit realm.

2. A Godly pastor (or shepherd) must be quick of _____.

3. One purpose of true prophetic revelation is to _____ the people of God.

Multiple Choice — Choose the best answer from the list below:

    A. demons   C. liberty

    B. God   D. Godliness

4. Some predictive prophetic words from _____ may not come to pass.

5. One hallmark of true revelation given by the Holy Spirit is that it produces _____.

Continued on the next page.

True or False

6. True revelation from the Holy Spirit will always produce life, not death. _____

7. We must test every spiritual revelation to discern its source. _____

8. When dealing directly with unclean/evil spirits we should confront them as soon as we sense them. _____

Scripture Memorization

9. Write out I John 4:2-3 and memorize it.

10. What was the primary insight you gained from this lesson, and how will you apply it to your life?

Lesson Eight:
The Spirit of Deception:
Seductive and Manipulative

I. **TO WHAT ARE YOU GIVING YOUR ATTENTION?**

   A. **I Timothy 4:1 – Theme Scripture**
   "But the Spirit explicitly says that in later times some will fall away from the faith, paying attention to deceitful spirits and doctrines of demons..."

   B. **Review of the Theme Verse**
   1. The Holy Spirit forewarns
   2. That in the later times (this applies more today than ever!)
   3. Some will fall away from the faith (Alert: this is addressing believers.)
   4. Paying attention – becoming fixated upon
   5. Deceitful demonic spirits – lying, deceiving, seducing spirits
   6. Resulting in false doctrines inspired by demons
   7. Let's wake up and receive this warning today!

   C. **To Be Forewarned Is to Be Forearmed**
   You do not have to be deceived; you can be prepared! And you can prepare others!

II. **DISCERNING THE NATURE OF GOOD AND EVIL**

   A. **A Name Reveals the Nature**
   1. "In the spirit realm the name of an entity always corresponds to its nature."[10]
   2. *"Abraham called the name of that place The LORD Will Provide, as it is said to this day, "In the mount of the LORD it will be provided."* Genesis 22:14
   3. *"God said to Moses, "I AM WHO I AM"; and He said, "Thus you shall say to the sons of Israel, 'I AM has sent me to you.'"* Exodus 3:14
   4. Note the many compound names of God. They each reveal a specific aspect of the nature of God. (Examples: Jehovah Rapha—The Lord Who Heals; Jehovah Jireh—The Lord Who Provides; Jehovah Nissi—The Lord Our Banner, etc.)

B. This Principle Is True for Evil Spirits as Well
1. To be effective in spiritual warfare, you must know the name of your enemy!
2. The term "unclean spirit" is used in both a generic and a specific sense.
   (See Zechariah 13:2, Matthew 12:43, Mark 1:23 and 26, Mark 3:30, Mark 5:2, Mark 5:8, Mark 7:25, Mark 9:25, Luke 8:29, Luke 9:42, Luke 11:24 and Revelation 18:2.)
3. According to Mark 5:6-9, the name "Legion" is used in Jesus' deliverance ministry as it reveals the nature of the demonic force, *"For we are many."*
4. From Revelation 9:11 it states, *"They have as king over them, the angel of the abyss; his name in Hebrew is Abaddon, and in the Greek he has the name Apollyon."* In English, these names mean "Destruction and Destroyer." The names reveal the nature.

C. Walking the Balance Beam!
1. We are followers of Christ, not the devil. Revelation 19:14 states, *"the armies which are in heaven... were following Him."*
2. Likewise, true disciples follow the Lamb wherever He goes. Revelation 14:4 states, *"These are the ones who have not been defiled with women, for they have kept themselves chaste. These are the ones who follow the Lamb wherever He goes. These have been purchased from among men as first fruits to God and to the Lamb."*

III. DECEITFUL SPIRITS LURKING IN THE SHADOWS

A. Demonic Spirits Attempt to Hide Their True Nature
James 1:16-17 – *"Do not be deceived, my beloved brethren. Every good thing given and every perfect gift is from above, coming down from the Father of lights, with whom there is no variation or shifting shadow."*

B. They Are Seductive in Nature
When considering the term "seductive", we often think only in terms of sexual activity. To seduce someone is to draw them from a place of security into a place of instability, then to vulnerability and ultimately into deception.

C. They Are Manipulative in Nature

Demonic spirits attempt to hide their true identity and motivation. All demonic spirits act according to the nature of their leader, Satan. They attempt manipulate a person by cunning tricks to eventually capture their will, lure them from walking in the light into practicing in the shadows, and ultimately into the utter depths of darkness.

D. We Must Walk in the Light
1. *"Jesus answered, 'Are there not twelve hours in the day? If anyone walks in the day, he does not stumble, because he sees the light of this world.'"* John 11:9
2. *"The night is almost gone, and the day is near. Therefore let us lay aside the deeds of darkness and put on the armor of light."* Romans 13:12
3. *"You are all children of the light and children of the day. We do not belong to the night or to the darkness."* I Thes. 5:5 NIV

IV. DOCTRINES OF DEMONS

A. Error by Exaggeration – Truth Wrapped in a Lie
1. Something may begin as a truth by the Spirit of God (See Galatians 3:1-5) and then become distorted by additives.
2. The enemy attempts to add or amplify soulish elements to the truth especially concerning identity issues of insecurity or unhealed wounds. This can result in a misplaced emphasis.
3. This can cause what began as a truth to subtly become an error!

B. Error by Exalting a Special Revelation Above the Word of God
1. This can sound like, "But you do not understand. This teaching came to me by an angel." (See Colossians 2:18-19)
2. Or you might hear something like, "That is *elementary*—what I am offering you is *special*!"
3. Eventually it results in adding extra books on the same level of authority of the Scriptures—the Word of God. (Consider the warning of Galatians 1:6-9.)

C. Error by Prideful Promoting of Self into an Elitist Position
1. This includes those who become too big in their own eyes to fellowship with different streams and exclusivity occurs.
2. Scripture warns us not to forsake the assembling of believers (See Hebrews 10:23-25).
3. When this occurs, a person is then no longer accountable.

D. Error of Entering into Hero Worship
1. There are those who wrongly state that they are the "Elijah" that must come before the Coming of the Messiah.
2. Believers wrongly become enamored by big gifts.
3. Too many people with seared consciences, following doctrines of demons, worshipping man and not God alone.

V. WALKING IN THE OPPOSITE SPIRIT
We are never too old for the Sermon on the Mount of the teachings of Jesus as found in Matthew chapters 5, 6 and 7. We must learn to walk in the opposite spirit and in the nature of Christ Jesus. What Would Jesus Do?

A. Peace Must Rule Our Hearts – Colossians 3:15
"Let the peace of Christ rule in your hearts, to which indeed you were called in one body; and be thankful."

B. Abounding in Love – Philippians 1:9
"And this I pray, that your love may abound still more and more in real knowledge and all discernment."

C. Made Complete in Christ – Colossians 2:9-10
"For in Him all the fullness of Deity dwells in bodily form, and in Him you have been made complete, and He is the head over all rule and authority;"

VI. GLEANINGS FROM THE LIFE OF MICHAEL BROWN

A. Dr. Michael Brown's Background
Dr. Michael Brown is a scholar in the Body of Christ who is Jewish in his background and found Jesus as his Messiah. He is a trusted teacher, author, revivalist, equipper, debater and cultural commentator in our day.

B. The Torch Bearer of Truth
Dr. Michael Brown, scholar and theologian, gives us insight in his book, *Let No One Deceive You*: "According to the New Testament, the possibility of deception is very real. But that does not mean that everyone has to be deceived! We can be kept safe in Jesus. The Lord can bring us into a wide place where we can be firmly rooted and secure, and it is for that very reason the Bible often says to us: "Be not deceived."[11]

C. Personal Goal
One of my goals is that I want to be a person who by grace starts well, but also finishes well. In order for that to occur, I must be a person who walks in discernment and avoids the deception of the powers of darkness.

VII. JOIN ME IN PRAYER TO WALK IN THE LIGHT

A. Rescue the Perishing – Care for the Dying[12]
This is another old popular hymn. It lyrically carries a burden for those who have lost their way. We each need to carry this burden of the Lord in a prayerful and worshipful manner. Remember, we are to be worshippers of God and then deliverers of men. Amen and Amen!

B. An Invitation to Walk in the Light
Join me in an invitation to Step into the Light of God's Word, Will and Ways and out of the shadows of seductive and manipulative deception.

C. Let's Pray Together!
Gracious Father, in Jesus' mighty name, we thank you for the light of Your Word being granted to us. We admit our need and our total dependency upon You. If there is any form of deception in our lives, we ask that the Holy Spirit release conviction, revelation, discernment and freedom to us and our families. We choose to come out of alliance with any form of darkness and step into proper alignment with the ways of God. We worship You. We thank You. We magnify Your great name! This is a day of salvation and we will greatly rejoice! Amen and Amen.

Reflection Questions
Lesson Eight: The Spirit of Deception: Seductive and Manipulative

Answers to these questions can be found in the back of the study guide.

Fill in the Blank

1. List three areas that are considered doctrines of demons.

   1. _____ 2. _____ 3. _____

2. Our _____ are not a measure of our spiritual maturity.

3. In the spirit realm, the _____ of an entity always corresponds to its nature.

Multiple Choice — Choose the best answer from the list below:

   A. good   C. hide
   B. Show off   D. complete

4. A _____ defense against deception is to walk in humility.

5. Demonic spirits do their best to _____ their true identity.

Continued on the next page.

True or False

6. To be effective in spiritual warfare, it is helpful to know the name of our enemy. _____

7. Apostles and Prophets are accountable only to God. _____

8. If something contains truth, then it cannot also contain deception. _____

Scripture Memorization

9. Write out James 1:16-17 and memorize it.

10. What was the primary insight you gained from this lesson, and how will you apply it to your life?

Lesson Nine:
Exposing Demonic Influences:
Setting the Captives Free

I. **HE CAME TO SET THE CAPTIVES FREE!**

   A. **Luke 4:17-20 – Theme Scripture**
   "And the book of the prophet Isaiah was handed to Him. And He opened the book and found the place where it was written, "THE SPIRIT OF THE LORD IS UPON ME, BECAUSE HE ANOINTED ME TO PREACH THE GOSPEL TO THE POOR. HE HAS SENT ME TO PROCLAIM RELEASE TO THE CAPTIVES, AND RECOVERY OF SIGHT TO THE BLIND, TO SET FREE THOSE WHO ARE OPPRESSED, TO PROCLAIM THE FAVORABLE YEAR OF THE LORD." And He closed the book, gave it back to the attendant and sat down; and the eyes of all in the synagogue were fixed on Him."

   B. **Jesus Is Commissioned and He Commissions**
   1. The Spirit of the Lord is upon me
   2. The Spirit of the Lord has anointed me
   3. The Spirit of the Lord has empowered me with Good News
   4. The Spirit of the Lord has sent me to the poor
   5. The Spirit of the Lord is releasing captives through me
   6. The Spirit of the Lord is giving sight to those around me
   7. The Spirit of the Lord is setting free those who are oppressed
   8. The Spirit of the Lord is declaring it is a time of favor

   C. **Impacted by Mike Bickle of IHOP-KC**
   "I am called to be a worshipper of God and a deliverer of men." The order of this purpose statement by Mike Bickle is extremely important to note.

   D. **My Eventual Revelation and Conviction**
   My prayer has become the following, "I ask the Holy Spirit to cast light on the hindrances that keep me from receiving and discerning revelation and then acting upon it. As I am set free, I am empowered to give away what I have received."

II. EXPOSING THE RELIGIOUS SPIRIT

A. Primary Scriptures – II Timothy 3:1, 5 & Matthew 16:6
1. *"But realize this, that in the last days difficult times will come… holding to a form of godliness, although they have denied its power; avoid such as these."* II Timothy 3:1, 5
2. *"And Jesus said to them, "Watch out and beware of the leaven of the Pharisees and Sadducees."* Matthew 16:6

B. Primary Insight Granted
"A religious spirit is a demon that seeks to substitute religious activity for the power of the Holy Spirit in our lives."[13]

1. The religious spirit promotes a works-based or a performance-based acceptance rather than receiving approval through the cross of Jesus.
2. The three primary building blocks of the religious spirit are guilt, pride and fear.
3. When a religious sprit is founded upon pride, it is evidenced by perfectionism.

C. Write Out a Brief Testimony or Example of This Teaching

_____

_____

_____

_____

III. EXPOSING THE POLITICAL SPIRIT

A. Primary Scriptures – Mark 3:6 & Luke 23:9-11
1. *"The Pharisees went out and immediately began conspiring with the Herodians against Him, as to how they might destroy Him."* Mark 3:6
2. *"And he questioned Him at some length; but He answered him nothing. And the chief priests and the scribes were standing there, accusing Him vehemently. And Herod with his soldiers, after treating Him with contempt and mocking Him, dressed Him in a gorgeous robe and sent Him back to Pilate."* Luke 23:9-11

B. Primary Insight Granted
1. The political spirit has hidden purposes and agendas that you will not be able to discern with your natural senses.
2. The political spirit is an invisible demonic mastermind that strategizes ways to kill God's authentic plans and purposes at any cost.
3. The political spirit often creates alliances with religious spirits and institutions backed by mammon to achieve its corrupt goals.
4. The political spirit will always try to buy off, corrupt, manipulate and eventually dominate leaders and groups of people to accomplish its desired result.
5. The political spirit mesmerizes people into false loyalties while issuing demands of uniformity through the pressures of fear, shame and control.

C. Write Out a Brief Testimony or Example of This Teaching

_____

_____

_____

_____

IV. EXPOSING THE SPIRIT OF FEAR & INTIMIDATION

A. Primary Scriptures – II Timothy 1:7 & Joshua 10:25
1. *"For God has not given us a spirit of timidity, but of power and love and discipline."* II Timothy 1:7
2. *"Joshua then said to them, "Do not fear or be dismayed! Be strong and courageous, for thus the LORD will do to all your enemies with whom you fight."* Joshua 10:25

B. Primary Insight Granted
1. Faith propels you and fear paralyzes you.
2. Fear belittles you and causes you to look at your own inadequacies instead of looking to God for His empowerment.
3. The spirit of intimidation holds people in its prey by controlling them with threats and consequences.

C. Write Out a Brief Testimony or Example of This Teaching

_____

_____

_____

_____

V. EXPOSING THE SPIRIT OF ANTICHRIST

A. Primary Scriptures – I John 2:18-19 & 4:2-3
1. *"Children, it is the last hour; and just as you heard that antichrist is coming, even now many antichrists have appeared; from this we know that it is the last hour. They went out from us, but they were not really of us; for if they had been of us, they would have remained with us; but they went out, so that it would be shown that they all are not of us."* I John 2:18-19
2. *"By this you know the Spirit of God: every spirit that confesses that Jesus Christ has come in the flesh is from God; and every spirit that does not confess Jesus is not from God; this is the spirit of the antichrist, of which you have heard that it is coming, and now it is already in the world."* I John 4:2-3

B. Primary Insight Granted
1. The first key word to understand here is the word "*anti.*" It means "against" and/or "in place of."
2. The second word to understand here is the word "*Christ.*" This comes from the Greek word *cristos* meaning the meaning "the anointed one."
3. Thus the literal anti-Christ comes against Christ and sets himself up in place of Him. The spirit of anti-Christ acts after the nature of the anti-Christ: it comes against the anointed ones and comes to replace them with a false anointing.

C. Write Out a Brief Testimony or Example of This Teaching

VI. WISDOM FROM THE LIFE AND MINISTRY OF FRANCIS FRANGIPANE

A. Francis Frangipane's Background
Francis Frangipane has been a pastor, an intercessor and one of the clearest apostolic teaching voices in this generation. After ministering in the state of Iowa for years, and serving as an adviser to numerous ministries, he now devotes his time to prayer, study and writing.

B. Lessons from *The Three Battlegrounds*
In his book, *The Three Battlegrounds*, Francis Frangipane breaks spiritual warfare down into three primary fronts: your own mind, the church, and the wider unseen supernatural reality. Only after you discern a demonic influence in your own life and conquer it in the power of Jesus, can you realistically advance to the next battleground or sphere of authority. Eventually, you may gain enough experiential authority to effectively handle your part of the battle on a city and even global front.[14]

C. Wisdom I Have Gleaned – No Common Ground Allowed
"I will not speak much more with you, for the ruler of the world is coming, and he has nothing in Me..." John 14:30

I teach about the concept of "No Common Ground Allowed," as referenced in this scripture, in my Study Guide and Class called *Prayers that Strike the Mark*. Please see those complimentary teaching materials as they are supportive to this subject.[15]

VII. JOIN ME IN PRAYER TO SET THE CAPTIVES FREE

A. You Are My Hiding Place[16]
This worship song is based from Psalm 91. Yes, He is our hiding place. This amazing devotional scripture in song helps us to keep things in a right priority.

B. An Invitation to be a Worshipper of God and Deliverer of Men
Some things are worth repeating and this principle that I learned from Mike Bickle from the International House of Prayer in Kansas City is one of them. We are called first to be worshippers of God and then empowered to be deliverers of men. Amen!

C. Let's Pray Together!
Heavenly Father, in Jesus' name, we worship You and enthrone You with our praises. According to your Word, Jesus came to set the captives free and declare the favorable year of the Lord. As ambassadors of Christ, we believe the Holy Spirit has anointed us to be worshippers of God and deliverers of men. Once again, we surrender to You all that we are and all that we hope to be. Anoint us with higher levels of discernment so we can know the motivating spirit behind an activity. By the grace of God, we believe that we are receiving an increase of Your revelatory ways in our lives for Your Kingdom's sake. Amen and Amen.

Reflection Questions
Lesson Nine: Exposing Demonic Influences: Setting the Captives Free

Answers to these questions can be found in the back of the study guide.

Fill in the Blank

1. The anti-christ attempts to set up false _____ to replace true _____.

2. List four things that Jesus commissions us to do.
   1. _____ 3. _____
   2. _____ 4. _____

3. The _____ and _____ spirits often create alliances to gain control of institutions.

Multiple Choice — Choose the best answer from the list below:

   A. inferiority   C. pride
   B. intimidation   D. mammon

4. When a religious sprit is founded upon _____, it is evidenced by perfectionism.

5. The spirit of _____ holds others in its prey by controlling them with threats and consequences.

Continued on the next page.

True or False

6. The religious spirit promotes a works-based or a performance-based acceptance. _____

7. Political and religious spirits should be exposed, confronted and rebuked as soon as they are discerned. _____

8. "No Common Ground" generally refers to the idea that we must have nothing in common with the spiritual force we are confronting. _____

Scripture Memorization

9. Write out I John 4:2-3 and memorize it.

10. What was the primary insight you gained from this lesson, and how will you apply it to your life?

Lesson Ten:
Staying Out of Satan's Traps:
Wisdom to Avoid Common Pitfalls

I. **MASQUERADE AND DISGUISE PARTIES!**

   A. **II Corinthians 11:13-15 – Theme Scripture**
   "For such men are false apostles, deceitful workers, disguising themselves as apostles of Christ. No wonder, for even Satan disguises himself as an angel of light. Therefore it is not surprising if his servants also disguise themselves as servants of righteousness, whose end will be according to their deeds."

   B. **Jesus Is Commissioned and He Commissions**
   1. God is the Creator
   2. Satan is an Imitator
   3. God has the Original
   4. Satan has a Distorted Copy
   5. God is the Author of the Real
   6. Satan is the Author of the False
   7. God is Light and the Source of Light
   8. Satan Disguises himself as an Angel of Light
   9. God has Righteous Servants
   10. Satan inspires a Masquerade Party

   C. **I Am to Discern Good and Evil**
   I am to be so in tune with the truth and source of light, that as a result I can see, hear, feel, taste, smell, and know the difference between the whole truth and a partial truth (subtle lie).

   D. **My Ultimate Conviction**
   "I am to walk so closely with the Holy Spirit that together we can detect a lie disguised as truth, flushing out darkness by emanating the Light of God into every sphere of life."

II. **EXPOSING THE JEZEBEL AND AHAB INFLUENCE**

   A. **Primary Scriptures – I Kings 21:25 & Revelation 2:19-20**
   1. *"Surely there was no one like Ahab who sold himself to do evil in the sight of the LORD, because Jezebel his wife incited him."* I Kings 21:25

2. *"I know your deeds, and your love and faith and service and perseverance, and that your deeds of late are greater than at first. But I have this against you, that you tolerate the woman Jezebel, who calls herself a prophetess, and she teaches and leads My bond-servants astray so that they commit acts of immorality and eat things sacrificed to idols."* Revelation 2:19-20

B. Primary Insights on Jezebel and Ahab

"Witchcraft is counterfeit spiritual authority; it is using a spirit other than the Holy Spirit to dominate, manipulate, or control others." [17]

1. Jezebel is a prime example of witchcraft in the scriptures. She used her power to control her husband Ahab, the King, and thus she was the one who had the ultimate authority over Israel.
2. Jezebel's soulish and demonic assault (and that of the spirit of witchcraft) often comes in a series of successive stings to weaken the one in position.
3. These stunning stings may result in: discouragement, confusion, depression, loss of vision, disorientation, withdrawal, despair and defeat.
4. Dr. Lester Sumrall taught that there are seven stages of demonic influence: regression, repression, suppression, depression, oppression, obsession and possession.
5. It is ultimately a battle of true and false authority; who will rule and reign. But Romans 16:20 states, *"The God of Peace will soon crush Satan under your feet."*

C. Write Out a Brief Testimony or Example of This Teaching

_____

_____

_____

_____

III. AVOIDING SATAN'S PRIDEFUL SCHEMES

A. Primary Scriptures – Job 41:1-10, Isaiah 27:1, James 4:6 & I Peter 5:5

1. *"Can you draw out Leviathan with a fishhook? Or press down his tongue with a cord? Can you put a rope in his nose or pierce his jaw with a hook? Will he make many supplications to you, or will he speak to you soft words? Will he make a covenant with you? Will you take him for a servant forever? Will you play with him as with a bird, or will you bind him for your maidens? Will the traders bargain over him? Will they divide him among the merchants? Can you fill his skin with harpoons, or his head with fishing spears? Lay your hand on him; remember the battle; you will not do it again! Behold, your expectation is false; will you be laid low even at the sight of him? No one is so fierce that he dares to arouse him; who then is he that can stand before Me?"* Job 41:1-10

2. *"In that day the LORD will punish Leviathan the fleeing serpent, with His fierce and great and mighty sword, even Leviathan the twisted serpent; and He will kill the dragon who lives in the sea."* Isaiah 27:1

3. *"But he gives us more grace. That is why Scripture says: 'God opposes the proud but shows favor to the humble.'"* James 4:6

4. *"All of you, clothe yourselves with humility toward one another, because, 'God opposes the proud but shows favor to the humble.'"* I Peter 5:5b

B. Primary Insights on Pride and Leviathan

1. Pride comes before a fall.
2. We are called to humble ourselves.
3. Leviathan is a strong demonic spirit that is motivated by extreme pride.
4. Leviathan twists communications and causes people to have muffled hearing, resulting in a form of a deaf and dumb spirit.
5. This spirit of pride illustrated by Leviathan converges with the religious and political spirits and is often involved in the relationships of an Ahab and Jezebel, using cunning speech to manipulate its prey.

C. Write Out a Brief Testimony or Example of This Teaching

_____

_____

_____

_____

IV. EXPOSING THE SPIRIT OF OFFENSE

A. Primary Scriptures – Luke 17:1 & II Timothy 2:24-26
1. *"He said to His disciples, 'It is inevitable that stumbling blocks come, but woe to him through whom they come!'"* Luke 17:1
2. *"The Lord's bond-servant must not be quarrelsome, but be kind to all, able to teach, patient when wronged, with gentleness correcting those who are in opposition, if perhaps God may grant them repentance leading to the knowledge of the truth, and they may come to their senses and escape from the snare of the devil, having been held captive by him to do his will."* II Tim. 2:24-26

B. Primary Insights on Offense*
1. The Greek word for "offend" in Luke 17:1 comes from the word *skandalon*. This word originally referred to the part of a trap to which the bait was attached.
2. Those who are in quarrels or opposition fall into a trap and are held prisoner to do the devil's will. Even more alarming, they are most often unaware of their captivity!
3. There are two major categories into which offended people can be divided: 1) those who have been treated unjustly, and 2) those who believe with all their hearts that they have been wronged. They judge by assumption, appearance, and hearsay.

*This material is inspired from *The Bait of Satan* book by John Bevere.[18]

C. Write Out a Brief Testimony or Example of This Teaching

_____

_____

_____

_____

V. THE ENEMY'S PLAN VS. GOD'S PLAN

A. An Overview of the Enemy's Plan
Satan has established a rival spiritual kingdom in opposition to God, ruling over fallen angels operating (possibly) in the heavenlies and demonic spirits on earth. Satan's objectives are to rob the Son of God of His place with the Father and the honor that is due Him from the people of earth. The enemy's goal is to gain as much control of the world's system as possible and to receive universal worship for himself. Remember: All true spiritual warfare centers around the placement of the Son.[19]

B. An Overview of God's Plan
God's objectives on earth are to reap the earth's last great harvest of souls and to prepare the bride as a gift for His Son. Christ, then, has committed to His disciples two special responsibilities: to restrain Satan on earth until God's purposes of grace have been fulfilled; and, according to some interpretations, to cast down (wage war, wrestle with) Satan's kingdom set up in the heavenlies.[20]

C. Jesus Transfers His Authority to His Followers*
"Then Jesus came to them and said, "All authority in heaven and on earth has been given to me." Matthew 28:18 NIV
1. Romans 3:23; 6:23; 5:8 – Jesus paid the ransom for man's soul, which was proclaimed by God in Genesis 2:17 (bought back His Lordship).
2. Galatians 3:13-14 – Jesus redeemed (sinless man for sin-filled men); the price was paid.
3. Colossians 2:15; Ephesians 4:8-9 – Jesus triumphed over Satan and all authorities. He disarmed and displayed the defeated.
4. Ephesians 1:17-22 – Jesus is over all!
5. Matthew 28:19-20 – Now we go forth as His ambassadors.

6. I John 4:4 – We carry the revelation that greater is He that is in us than the one in the world!
7. James 4:7 – Submitting requires humility; then we resist and the enemy has to flee!
8. Mark 16:17 – In the great commission we are called to cast out demons!

* This section is expanded on in my *Deliverance from Darkness Study Guide*.[21]

VI. INSIGHT FROM THE LIFE AND MINISTRY OF JOHN BEVERE

A. John Bevere's Background
John Bevere, along with his wife, Lisa, are some of the most influential and strategic leaders in the body of Christ today. Their personal testimony includes coming victoriously through a situation of serious offense. They removed themselves from the polluting influences and learned how to forgive completely. John teaches, by walking in forgiveness we can deprive the enemy of "landing strips" in our soul. Forgiveness is a potent antidote to the demonic toxins that could otherwise bring you down to the enemy's level.

B. Lessons from *The Bait of Satan* & *Breaking Intimidation*
As John pointed out in his book, *The Bait of Satan*, "One of the most deceptive and insidious kids of bait is something every Christian has encountered—offense. Actually, offense is not deadly—if it stays in the trap. But if we pick it up and consume it and feed on it in our hearts, then we have become offended."[22]

C. The Key to Staying Clean
Walking in forgiveness is the primary key to keep yourself clean with no landing strip for the demonic to have a foothold. Forgiveness is a lifestyle. In Jesus' model prayer, he encourages us to pray this as long as it is called today.

VII. JOIN ME IN PRAYER FOR GREATER WISDOM

A. Draw Me Nearer, Nearer Precious Lord[23]
Do you want to stay out of Satan's traps and snares? Then join me in the lyrics of another doctrinally amazing old hymn and draw close to God. After the all, the Heart of God is the safest place you can be!

B. An Invitation for the Added Ingredient of Wisdom
Along with our passion, zeal and knowledge, let's add the often-missing ingredient of the wisdom ways of God. Join me in asking the Holy Spirit to teach us His Wisdom Ways.

C. Let's Pray Together!

Heavenly Father, in Jesus' name, as ambassadors of Christ, we agree that we are called to set the captives free and to enforce the victory of Calvary. We ask for wisdom beyond our years to be able to avoid common pitfalls of the enemy. Thank You for exposing the plots of Ahab and Jezebel, Leviathan and his prideful ways, and the spirit of offense. We surrender our pasts, our present and all that we hope to be to You. Release higher levels of discernment so we can exercise Kingdom authority and dislodge any hindrances that stand in the way of us operating in a higher form of pure revelation. Praise the Lord! Amen and Amen.

Reflection Questions
Lesson Ten: Staying Out of Satan's Traps: Wisdom to Avoid Common Pitfalls

Answers to these questions can be found in the back of the study guide.

Fill in the Blank

1. Our spiritual senses are to be so conditioned to God's nature that _____ is easily discerned.

2. Witchcraft is counterfeit spiritual _____.

3. Part of our responsibility as Christians is to _____ Satan on earth until God's purposes of grace have been fulfilled.

Multiple Choice — Choose the best answer from the list below:

    A.   worship   C.   primary

    B.   glory   D.   universal

4. Walking in forgiveness is the _____ key to keeping yourself clean.

5. The enemy's goal is to gain control of the world's system and to receive universal _____ for himself.

Continued on the next page.

True or False

6. Witchcraft is a spirit that seeks to dominate, manipulate, or control others. _____

7. When I am in tune with the truth and source of light, I can easily discern good and evil. _____

8. Humility and keeping our focus on Christ will keep us from the traps of the enemy. _____

Scripture Memorization

9. Write out II Corinthians 11:13-15 and memorize it.

10. What was the primary insight you gained from this lesson, and how will you apply it to your life?

Lesson Eleven:
Creating a Culture of Faith:
Ingredients for a Safe House

I. ASSURANCE IN TIMES OF TROUBLE

A. I John 5:4b – Theme Scripture
"This is the victory that has overcome the world, even our faith."

B. Jesus Has Won the Victory
1. On the cross, Jesus said, *"It is finished."*
2. Therefore, the victory of Christ has already been accomplished.
3. Christ has overcome the world's system of darkness.
4. As believers, we are invited to be overcomers with Christ Jesus.
5. We are engaged in an ongoing battle between good and evil.
6. Faith in God displaces the evil culture of fear every time.
7. Our faith, together, enforces the victory of Calvary.
8. Our prayer is for His Kingdom to come on earth as it is in heaven.

C. Am I Creating a Culture of Fear or Faith?
This is one of the most challenging questions to answer in our day. Jesus warned that many hearts will fail due to fear (Luke 21:26). What is to be our response in these days, and in our personal lives? How can we make a difference? Are we creating a culture of fear or faith? How do we build a safe house?

D. A Personal Word I Did Not Fully Understand
"Your end time worldview will determine your lifestyle." The Holy Spirit spoke this word to me while I was a young pastor. It has stuck with me all my life. At the time I did not understand the word and certainly did not have the right interpretation or application to this piercing statement. Today, I know this is a certain truth, *"Your end time worldview will determine your lifestyle."*

II. RESHAPING MY THINKING TO A BIBLICAL WORLDVIEW

A. Align to Four Important Core Values
1. God is good all the time.
2. Nothing is impossible with God.
3. Everything that needed to be accomplished was completed at Cross of Calvary.
4. As ambassadors of Christ we carry His delegated regal authority.

B. Healthy Attitudes and Applications
These three values shape your attitudes and expectations.
1. We do not fight towards victory; we fight from victory.
2. False humility will deny your destiny, but true humility will take you to it.
3. Our boasting should be in what Christ has already accomplished, not in our ability to bring His earthly rule and reign to pass.

C. The Isaiah 60:1-3 Template
"Arise, shine; for your light has come, and the glory of the LORD has risen upon you. For behold, darkness will cover the earth and deep darkness the peoples; But the LORD will rise upon you and His glory will appear upon you. Nations will come to your light, and kings to the brightness of your rising."
1. Historically, this passage has already transpired. This is a "Messianic Prophecy" concerning the coming of Jesus, the Son of God. Kings have already come to the brightness of His shining (see Matthew 2:1).
2. Jesus the Messiah is the "Light of the World" (see John 8:12; 9:5).
3. When the historical (past), present, and future interpretations and applications of these verses are all brought together, they result in the fullness.
4. We are told to, "Arise, shine." We are not told to only, "Gaze, reflect."
5. We must do our part! We must not deny that "darkness will cover the earth." But we must deny its finality. Darkness does not have the final say!
6. Therefore, we must arise and let His shining light within us (see Colossians 1:27) displace the evil around us.
7. His glory will appear and eventually cover the earth! We are invited to participate in "Glorious Eschatology."

III. WALKING IN THE AUTHORITY OF THE WORD OF GOD*

A. God Transferred Authority (Not Ownership) To Man
1. Genesis 1:26, 28 – Subdue and have dominion (authority to act) over all things. ("Let us... let them" = It is God's to give).
2. Exact likeness (holy, sinless and with delegated authority).

B. **Transfer of Authority from Man to Satan**
Luke 4:6 – *And he said to him, "I will give you all their authority and splendor, for it has been given to me, and I can give it to anyone I want to."*
1. Genesis 2:17; 3:6-11, 22-23 – Disobedience caused separation between God and man.
2. Willful obedience to Satan – Adam and Eve knew God's word but chose to disobey it. See Romans 6:16 – slaves obeying a master.
3. II Corinthians 4:4 – god (magistrate—not the owner) of this world age or time period, which is limited and temporary.
4. Ephesians 2:2 – Prince of the power of the air has been given the temporary right to act in the atmosphere.

C. **Authority Transferred to Jesus**
Matthew 28:18 – *Then Jesus came to them and said, "All authority in heaven and on earth has been given to me."* NIV
1. Romans 3:23; 6:23; 5:8 – Jesus paid the ransom for man's soul, which was proclaimed by God in Genesis 2:17 (bought back His Lordship).
2. Galatians 3:13-14 – Jesus redeemed (one sinless man for all sin-filled men)—the price was paid.
3. Colossians 2:15; Ephesians 4:8-9 – Jesus triumphed over Satan and all authorities. Jesus disarmed the powers and openly displayed their defeat.
4. Ephesians 1:17-22 – Jesus is over all. We must come into alignment with this reality.

D. **Jesus Transfers Authority to Believers**
1. Holy, sinless authority was made available again!
   a) Same breath – Genesis 2:2; John 20:20-22
   b) Same power – Acts 1:8; Luke 24:47
2. Ephesians 1:22b – He gave us all.
3. Matthew 28:19-20 – Now we go.
4. I John 4:4 – Greater is He Who is in us!
5. James 4:7 – Submitting requires humility, then we take a stand and resist the evil and it must flee!
6. Mark 16:17 – We are called to cast out demons!

* This section is also found and expanded on, in my study guide, *Deliverance from Darkness*.[24]

IV. WALKING IN COMMUNITY – WE ARE BETTER TOGETHER

A. We Are God's Building
I Corinthians 3:9-10 – *"For we are God's fellow workers; you are God's field, God's building. According to the grace of God which was given to me, like a wise master builder I laid a foundation, and another is building on it. But each man must be careful how he builds on it."*

B. Built Together for a Habitation of God
Ephesians 2:22 – *"In whom you also are being built together into a dwelling of God in the Spirit."*

C. Firmly Rooted and Built Up in Him
Colossians 2:6-7 – *"Therefore as you have received Christ Jesus the Lord, so walk in Him, having been firmly rooted and now being built up in Him and established in your faith, just as you were instructed, and overflowing with gratitude."*

D. The Power of a Three-Cord Strand
Ecclesiastes 4:12 – *"And if one can overpower him who is alone, two can resist him. A cord of three strands is not quickly torn apart."*

E. Greater Faith Together
I John 5:4b – *"This is the victory that has overcome the world, even our faith."*

V. WALKING IN THE POWER OF PROCLAMATION
"It is time to make a worldwide impact by calling forth the watchmen to the prophetic power of proclamation."

A. Proclamation Defined:
The meaning of proclamation is to proclaim, announce, declare, ascribe, call out, cry, invite, preach, pronounce, publish, read and herald.

B. Primary Scripture Verses and Principles

1. Deuteronomy 32:3-4
   "I will proclaim the name of the Lord. Oh, praise the greatness of our God! He is the Rock, his works are perfect, and all his ways are just. A faithful God who does no wrong, upright and just is he."

2. Isaiah 61:1-3
   "The Spirit of the Sovereign Lord is on me, because the Lord has anointed me to preach good news to the poor. He has sent me to bind up the brokenhearted, to proclaim freedom for the captives and release from darkness for the prisoners, to proclaim the year of the Lord's favor and the day of vengeance of our God, to comfort all who mourn, and provide for those who grieve in Zion— to bestow on them a crown of beauty instead of ashes, the oil of gladness instead of mourning, and a garment of praise instead of a spirit of despair. They will be called oaks of righteousness, a planting of the LORD for the display of his splendor."

3. What or Whom Do We Address in Proclamation?
   The power of proclamation, reminding and ascribing to God the greatness of His Name, isn't only in an intercessory orientation as in Deuteronomy 32:3-4. Neither is the power of proclamation only ministered through the praise warfare of ascribing greatness to His Name.

   In Isaiah 61, it is different. It is proclaiming liberty to the captives, freedom to the prisoners, proclaiming the favor of the Lord, releasing a mantle of praise and declaring destiny-seeing believers as oaks of righteousness. We release faith-filled proclamations to people, congregations, cities, etc. as the Holy Spirit directs.

4. Ephesians 5:19 and Colossians 3:16
   These scriptures talk of singing psalms, hymns, and spiritual songs to one another. The power to bless is in you and it is a privilege to be a mouthpiece of God to proclaim the power of the blessing and declare freedom to the captives. We are given the wonderful privilege to proclaim, to pronounce, to decree, to ascribe, to declare liberty and freedom to those in any form of bondage.

C. Turn on the Light!
Through the delegated authority given to us as believers we have the right to declare that light overcomes darkness. We help to create atmospheres that become saturated by God's glorious manifested presence. We are not just waiting to get out of the world; we are bringing God into the world. Light always overcomes darkness.

VI. INSIGHT FROM THE LIFE AND MINISTRY OF BILL JOHNSON

A. Bill Johnson's Background
Bill Johnson of Bethel Church in Redding, CA comes from a rich Pentecostal heritage with the grace of continuing to move forward in the things of God. Bill is one of the wisest men, who moves in authentic power, that I have ever had the joy of knowing.

B. Lessons from *God Is Good* and *Dreaming with God*
The Lord gives different revelations to His various leaders and believers. Bill Johnson helps us to understand that God wants to give us the "desires of our hearts," a reference from Psalm 37. Yet, we realize that as we make God our delight, He does a divine transfer where His heart becomes our heart, and thus our desires ultimately become His desires. God wants His people to live passionate, fulfilled lives where "Dreams Really Do Come True!" (For more on this subject see the books *Dreaming with God*[25] and *God is Good*[26] by Bill Johnson.)

C. God Has Invited Me to Dream with Him
"As a co-laborer with Christ, He invites me to dream with Him. God has a big dream in His heart that He wants to share with you and me. I must let the goodness of God permeate my heart and my mind. This then helps to shape my end time worldview and thus my way of living."

VII. JOIN ME IN PRAYER TO CREATE A CULTURE OF FAITH

A. Blessed Assurance, Jesus Is Mine![27]
Is there any truth greater than this? Oh the privilege, "To know Him and to be known by Him!" In creating an authentic culture of faith, we must always keep Jesus central in all things!

B. An Invitation to Create a Safe House of Faith
In my immediate family, creating and living in a "safe house" is a high priority. A safe house is one absent of the fear of man and the fear of rejection, and yet one in which stepping out in faith and even failing at times is not judged! Join me in praying that God will raise up many safe places where learning to step out in faith is celebrated and not judged. You can be part of the solution!

C. Let's Pray Together!

Gracious Father, we proclaim that we are better together. Together we have more faith, more power and more authority. We choose not to forsake the assembling of the saints and choose the way of love. We want Your house to be a safe house. Therefore, we renounce the spirit of fear and any past doctrines or associations that have promoted a culture of fear in our lives. We ask that the blood of Jesus cleanse us. Instead, we choose to walk in the opposite spirit. We declare ourselves to be Agents of Faith and clothe our minds with the goodness of God. Thank You in Jesus' name! Amen and Amen.

Reflection Questions
Lesson Eleven: Creating a Culture of Faith: Ingredients for a Safe House

Answers to these questions can be found in the back of the study guide.

Fill in the Blank

1. As a co-laborer with Christ, He invites me to _____ with Him.

2. Jesus transferred His _____ through the power of the Holy Spirit.

3. God's _____ will appear and eventually cover the earth!

Multiple Choice — Choose the best answer from the list below:

- A. delegated
- B. power
- C. love
- D. humility

4. As ambassadors of Christ we carry His _____ and regal authority.

5. False _____ will deny your destiny, but true _____ will take you to it.

Continued on the next page.

True or False

6. When we receive a word, we should release it as soon as possible. _____

7. In creating an authentic Culture of Faith, we must always keep Jesus central in all things. _____

8. When Adam sinned, his authority was transferred to Satan. _____

Scripture Memorization

9. Write out Colossians 2:6-7 and memorize it.

10. What was the primary insight you gained from this lesson, and how will you apply it to your life?

Lesson Twelve:
Revelation's Ultimate Purpose:
When the Word Becomes Flesh

I. **THE CALL TO INCARNATIONAL CHRISTIANITY!**

   A. **John 1:14 – Theme Scripture**
   "And the Word became flesh, and dwelt among us, and we saw His glory, glory as of the only begotten from the Father, full of grace and truth."

   B. **Jesus Is the Word Incarnate**
   1. Jesus is referred to as *"The Word."*
   2. *"The Word"* dwelt among us.
   3. We saw His Glory.
   4. Emphasizes that Jesus is the Only Son.
   5. *"The Word"*, Jesus, is full of grace and truth.

   C. **Ecclesiastes 4:12 – A Three Cord Strand: Being Like Christ**
   "And if one can overpower him who is alone, two can resist him. A cord of three strands is not quickly torn apart."
   1. Fullness of Gifting – The Power of the Holy Spirit Today
   2. Fullness of Fruit – The Character of Christ Today
   3. Fullness of Wisdom – The Mind of God Today

II. **THE PURPOSE OF PROPHETIC REVELATION**

   A. **Revelation 19:10 – It Releases the Testimony of Jesus**
   "Then I fell at his feet to worship him. But he said to me, 'Do not do that; I am a fellow servant of yours and your brethren who hold the testimony of Jesus; worship God. For the testimony of Jesus is the spirit of prophecy.'"

   1. To have a personal revelation of Jesus Christ is foundational to prophetic revelation.
   2. To know Him and to make Him known; to carry a testimony of Christ—this is the primary purpose of the prophetic.
   3. To know the future is not the primary focus of the prophetic.

B. Matthew 16:13-17 – It Releases a Revelation that Christ Is the Messiah
1. *"Jesus said to them (the Disciples) 'Who do you say that I am?'"* (Vs. 15).
2. *"And Simon Peter answered and said, 'Thou art the Christ, the Son of the living God'"* (Vs. 16).
3. *"Blessed are you, Simon Barjona, because flesh and blood did not reveal this to you, but My Father who is in heaven"* (Vs. 17).
4. Peter's bold confession of who Jesus was came by prophetic revelation, not by natural understanding.
5. It takes God to know God!

C. I Corinthians 12:3 – It Releases Revelation of the Lordship of Jesus

"Therefore I make known to you that no one speaking by the Spirit of God says, 'Jesus is accursed;' and no one can say, 'Jesus is Lord,' except by the Holy Spirit."

1. Paul said, no one can say "Jesus is Lord" except by the Holy Spirit.
2. The true prophetic purpose is to reveal the Lordship of Jesus.

D. True Prophetic Revelation Pierces Defenses
1. Read John 1:35-51 – In this passage Nathaniel's barriers are overcome by piercing revelation through Jesus' words of knowledge and discerning of spirits.
2. John 4:7-26 – In this interaction between Jesus and the woman at the well, we see a demonstration of how the prophetic pierces our defenses and barriers:
    a) She was a woman.
    b) She was met by a single man.
    c) They were not of the same race.
    d) She was a "half-breed" Samaritan.
    e) She worshipped false gods.
    f) She was an adulteress.
    g) She was deceitful, having lied and withheld the truth.
    h) True prophetic revelation broke down the defenses and she responded to His message.
    i) She acknowledged Him as a Prophet and recognized Him as the Messiah.

III. SPIRITUAL WARFARE - ACTING IN THE OPPOSITE SPIRIT

"Revelatory gifts are like anti-tank missiles used to shatter the enemy's schemes. They expose darkness and release freedom to the captives."

A. Romans 12:9-21 – The Goal of Spiritual Warfare: Overcome Evil with Good

"Let love be without hypocrisy. Abhor what is evil; cling to what is good. Be devoted to one another in brotherly love; give preference to one another in honor; not lagging behind in diligence, fervent in spirit, serving the Lord; rejoicing in hope, persevering in tribulation, devoted to prayer, contributing to the needs of the saints, practicing hospitality. Bless those who persecute you; bless and do not curse. Rejoice with those who rejoice, and weep with those who weep. Be of the same mind toward one another; do not be haughty in mind, but associate with the lowly. Do not be wise in your own estimation. Never pay back evil for evil to anyone. Respect what is right in the sight of all men. If possible, so far as it depends on you, be at peace with all men. Never take your own revenge, beloved, but leave room for the wrath of God, for it is written, "VENGEANCE IS MINE, I WILL REPAY," says the Lord. "BUT IF YOUR ENEMY IS HUNGRY, FEED HIM, AND IF HE IS THIRSTY, GIVE HIM A DRINK; FOR IN SO DOING YOU WILL HEAP BURNING COALS ON HIS HEAD." Do not be overcome by evil, but overcome evil with good."

B. Overcoming the Religious Spirit
1. Opinion is overcome by Truth with Knowledge
2. Legalism is overcome by Grace
3. Debate is overcome by Wise Speech
4. Criticism is overcome by Evaluation
5. Judgment is overcome by Blessing or Mercy

C. Walking in the Traits of the Zadok Priesthood – Ezekiel 44:15-23

"But the Levitical priests, the sons of Zadok, who kept charge of My sanctuary when the sons of Israel went astray from Me, shall come near to Me to minister to Me.... Linen turbans shall be on their heads and linen undergarments shall be on their loins; they shall not gird themselves with anything which makes them sweat... Moreover, they shall teach My people the difference between the holy and the profane, and cause them to discern between the unclean and the clean."

1. They shall come near to Me.
2. They are clothed in clean turbans and linen garments of righteousness.
3. They do nothing in their own strength—only that which is grace-empowered.

    4. They discern the difference between the holy and the profane.
    5. They are given the privilege to teach others how to discern between the unclean (evil) and clean (good).

  D. **Walking in the Spirit of Christ**
    1. Read Matthew 5-7 – The Sermon on the Mount: Words of Jesus by Which to Live.
    2. I was given a strategic dream stating, "You are never too old for the Sermon on the Mount."
    3. Walking in the Spirit and demonstrating the nature of Christ is one of the highest weapons of spiritual warfare.
    4. Battles of end time spiritual warfare will require that we walk with greater wisdom and increased discernment.

IV. **THE OF CULTURE HONOR**

  A. **Romans 12:10 – Preferring One Another**
  "Be devoted to one another in brotherly love; give preference to one another in honor;"

  B. **Matthew 10:41 – Receive a Prophet—Receive a Prophet's Reward**
  "He who receives a prophet in the name of a prophet shall receive a prophet's reward; and he who receives a righteous man in the name of a righteous man shall receive a righteous man's reward."

  C. **Personally Giving Honor to Whom Honor Is Due**
  Honoring some of the additional people that have impacted my life (These are listed in no particular order):

    1. C. Peter Wagner: shifting paradigms for the body of Christ
    2. Heidi Baker: stopping for the one; God is more than enough
    3. John Sanford: author of *The Elijah Task*; forerunner in merging the prophetic and healing graces
    4. Don Finto: great encourager and carrier of God's heart for Israel
    5. Jill Austin: demonstrated hunger for God; continually asked, "Are you satisfied or do you want more?"
    6. Che Ahn: preparing nets for the Harvest; a working model that family matters
    7. Mahesh Chavda: A life of prayer and fasting; Moving in the power of the Spirit with unusual discernment

V. COMMISSIONED TO BE AMBASSADORS OF HOPE
"To whom God willed to make known what is the riches of the glory of this mystery among the Gentiles, which is Christ in you, the hope of glory." Colossians 1:27

A. How We Obtain Hope
1. Romans 15:4 – Through perseverance and encouragement of the scriptures
2. Lamentations 3:21-23 – This I recall to my mind...
3. 1 Thessalonians 5:8 – Putting on the helmet of hope
4. Titus 2:13 – Looking for the blessed hope
5. Colossians 1:27 – Hope is a person

B. Benefits of Hope
1. Romans 15:4 – We are saved by hope
2. Romans 15:13 – We abound in hope
3. Ephesians 2:12 – The dramatic contrast
4. Ephesians 1:18 – Know the hope of His calling

C. I Corinthians 5:20 – The Calling of an Ambassador
"Therefore, we are ambassadors for Christ, as though God were making an appeal through us; we beg you on behalf of Christ, be reconciled to God."

VI. THE GLORIOUS BRIDE

A. A Look at the Future Bride of Christ
Ephesians 5:27 states, *"...that He might present to Himself the church in all her glory, having no spot or wrinkle or any such thing; but that she would be holy and blameless."*

B. Giants Cast Shadows for Us to Walk Within
Acts 5:15 inspires us with the following account, *"...to such an extent that they even carried the sick out into the streets and laid them on cots and pallets, so that when Peter came by at least his shadow might fall on any one of them."*

C. Is Your Shadow Dangerous?
"Is your shadow dangerous? Does it confront powers of darkness? Does your shadow of Christ result in the testimony of Jesus being released? Step out of any alliances with darkness and walk in the light? If so, you will cast the shadow of the Almighty and release the fragrance of Christ wherever you go!"

VII. JOIN ME IN PRAYER TO BECOME A WORD

A. A Mighty Fortress Is Our God[28]
One of the most famous and scripturally sound hymns in all of church history was composed by the reformer, Martin Luther. It is aptly titled "A Mighty Fortress is Our God." This hymn, like few others, exalts the nature of God Himself and enters into the power of declaration that God indeed is our Strong Tower.

B. An Invitation to Embody the Word
In closing this study, I want to invite us to do more than simply receive and discern revelation, but rather, become a word itself. Join me in this closing prayer.

C. Let's Pray Together!
Our Father, in Jesus' name, as New Testament believers, we desire to become a Living Word of God. We declare that we are becoming more mature by surrendering our senses to the Holy Spirit. By grace, we are growing in our discernment of good and evil. We want to cultivate a culture of Honor and to be authentic Ambassadors of Hope. We want to see a company of disciples of Jesus who embody the Word of God. Thank you for this opportunity to learn more and grow in grace and truth. Amen and Amen.

Reflection Questions
Lesson Twelve:
Revelation's Ultimate Purpose: When the Word Becomes Flesh

Answers to these questions can be found in the back of the study guide.

Fill in the Blank

1. True prophetic revelation will always contain the testimony of _____.

2. Prophetic revelation exposes _____ and releases freedom to the captives.

3. True _____ _____ breaks through defensive barriers.

Multiple Choice — Choose the best answer from the list below:

    A. honoring   C. true

    B. loving   D. primary

4. The _____ prophetic purpose is to reveal the Lordship of Jesus.

5. We can show the love of God by _____ one another.

Continued on the next page.

True or False

6. When we prophesy, we should strengthen, encourage, or comfort. _____

7. Spiritual warfare is in everything we do. _____

8. We are to learn and teach how to differentiate between the holy and profane. _____

Scripture Memorization

9. Write out Colossians 1:27 and memorize it.

10. What was the primary insight you gained from this lesson, and how will you apply it to your life?

Answers to the Reflection Questions

Lesson One: Surrendering Your Senses to the Holy Spirit
1. natural, spiritual
2. discernment, good, evil
3. the Holy Spirit
4. D. Practice
5. A. Discern
6. F   7. T   8. T

Lesson Two: Seeing: You Have More than One Set of Eyes
1. holy, profane
2. dreams, visions
3. journal or record
4. A. Rhema
5. C. Chozeh
6. T   7. F   8. F

Lesson Three: Hearing: Whatever He Hears, He Will Speak
1. cleansed
2. listening
3. friend
4. D. test it
5. B. hear
6. T   7. F   8. F

Lesson Four: Feeling: From the Heart Flows the Issues of Life
1. God
2. worship
3. emotions
4. A. burden
5. C. identity
6. T   7. F   8. T

Lesson Five: Tasting, Smelling & Other Leadings
1. spiritual
2. direction
3. C. sweet
4. A. smell
5. F   6. T   7. F

Lesson Six: Knowing: The Sixth Sense
1. Motivational
2. faith
3. Knowings
4. C. knowledge
5. A. solutions
6. T   7. F   8. T

The Discerner Study Guide
Answers to Reflection Questions

Lesson Seven: Testing the Spirits: Don't Believe Every Spirit!
1. test
2. scent
3. build up, admonish, or encourage (any or all)
4. B. God
5. C. liberty
6. T   7. T   8. F

Lesson Eight: The Spirit of Deception: Seductive and Manipulative
1. Any 3 of the following: Error by Exaggeration; Exalting a Special Revelation; Error by Prideful Promoting of Self; Error of Entering into Hero Worship
2. gifts
3. name
4. A. good
5. C. hide
6. T   7. F   8. F

Lesson Nine: Exposing Demonic Influences: Setting the Captives Free
1. anointings
2. Any of the Following: Empowered me with Good News; Sent me to the poor; Release captives through me; Give sight to those around me; Set free those who are oppressed; Declare it is a time of favor
3. political and religious
4. C. pride
5. B. intimidation
6. T   7. F   8. T

Lesson Ten: Avoiding Common Pitfalls: Wisdom from the Trenches
1. Evil
2. authority
3. restrain
4. C. primary
5. A. worship
6. T   7. T   8. T

Lesson Eleven: The Safety Net: Cultivating Faith Not Fear
1. dream
2. authority
3. glory
4. A. delegated
5. D. humility
6. F   7. T   8. T

Lesson Twelve: Revelation's Ultimate Purpose: When the Word Becomes Flesh
1. Jesus
2. darkness
3. Prophetic Revelation
4. C. true
5. A. honoring
6. T   7. T   8. T

Recommended Reading

Baker, Heidi. *Compelled by Love*. Lake Mary, FL: Charisma House, 2008.

Bevere, John. *The Bait of Satan*, 20th ann. ed. Lake Mary, FL: Charisma House, 2014.

Bolz, Shawn. *Translating God*. Self-published, 2015.

Brown, Michael L. *Let No One Deceive You*. Shippensburg, PA: Destiny Image, 1997.

Chavda, Mahesh. *Only Love Can Make a Miracle*. Self-published, 2002.

Chavda, Mahesh and Bonnie Chavda. *Watch of the Lord*. Lake Mary, FL: Charisma House, 1999.

Frangipane, Francis. *Discerning of Spirits*. Cedar Rapids, IA: Arrow Publications, 1994.

———. *The Three Battlegrounds*. Cedar Rapids, IA: Arrow Publications, 2006.

Hamon, Jane. *Dreams and Visions*, rev. ed. Bloomington, MN: Chosen Books, 2016.

Hotchkin, Robert. *Leviathan Exposed*. Maricopa, AZ: XP Publishing, 2016.

Jacobs, Cindy. *Deliver Us from Evil*. Ventura, CA: Regal Books [Gospel Light], 2010.

———. *The Voice of God* rev. ed. Bloomington, MN: Chosen Books, 2016.

Johnson, Bill. *God Is Good*. Shippensburg, PA: Destiny Image, 2016.

———. *The Supernatural Power of a Transformed Mind*, rev. ed. Shippensburg, PA: Destiny Image, 2014.

Joyner, Rick. *Overcoming Evil in the Last Days*, rev. ed. with study guide. Shippensburg, PA: Destiny Image, 2009.

———. *The Prophetic Ministry*. Fort Mill, SC: MorningStar Publications, 2006.

King, Patricia. *Eyes That See*, rev. ed. Maricopa, AZ: XP Publishing, 2010.

———. Developing Your Five Spiritual Senses. Maricopa, AZ: XP Publishing, 2014.

LeClaire, Jennifer. *The Spiritual Warrior's Guide to Defeating Jezebel*. Bloomington, MN: Chosen Books, 2013.

Malick, Faisal. *The Political Spirit*. Shippensburg, PA: Destiny Image, 2008.

Maloney, James. *The Panoramic Seer*. Shippensburg, PA: Destiny Image, 2012.

Nelson, Jerame. *Activating Your Spiritual Senses*. Self-published through Living at His Feet Publications, San Diego, CA, 2012.

Pierce, Chuck D. *Time to Defeat the Devil*. Lake Mary, FL: Charisma House, 2011.

——. *A Time to Triumph*. Bloomington, MN: Chosen Books, 2016.

Prince, Derek. *Blessing or Curse: You Can Choose*. Bloomington, MN: Chosen Books, 2006.

——. *They Shall Expel Demons*. Bloomington, MN: Chosen Books, 1998.

Robinson, Mickey. *The Prophetic Made Personal*. Shippensburg, PA: Destiny Image, 2010.

Sanford, John and Paula Sandford. *The Elijah Task*. Lake Mary, FL: Charisma House, 2006.

Sheets, Dutch. *Intercessory Prayer*. Bloomington, MN: Bethany House, 1996 [reprint edition 2016].

Smith, Laura Harris. *Seeing the Voice of God*. Bloomington, MN: Chosen Books, 2014.

Virkler, Mark and Patti. *Communion with God*. Shippensburg, PA: Destiny Image, 1991.

——. *Communion with God – Study Guide*. Shippensburg, PA: Destiny Image, 1991.

Wagner, C. Peter. *Freedom from the Religious Spirit*. Ventura, CA: Regal Books [Gospel Light], 2005.

Wagner, Doris M. *How to Cast Out Demons*. Ventura, CA: Renew Books [Gospel Light], 2000.

Welton, Jonathan. *The School of Seers*, rev. ed. Shippensburg, PA: Destiny Image, 2013.

Wimber, John. *Everyone Gets to Play*. Boise, ID: Ampelon Publishing, 2009.

Additional Resources by James W. Goll

(Many of these books feature a corresponding class and study guide and taught by James W. Goll, available at www.GodEncounters.com.)

Adventures in the Prophetic (with Michal Ann Goll, Mickey Robinson, Patricia King, Jeff Jansen, and Ryan Wyatt)

Angelic Encounters (with Michal Ann Goll)

The Call to the Elijah Revolution (with Lou Engle)

The Coming Israel Awakening

Deliverance from Darkness

The Discerner

Dream Language (with Michal Ann Goll)

Exploring Your Dreams and Visions

Finding Hope

God Encounters Today (with Michal Ann Goll)

Hearing God's Voice Today

The Lifestyle of a Prophet

The Lifestyle of a Watchman

The Lost Art of Intercession

The Lost Art of Practicing His Presence

The Lost Art of Pure Worship (with Chris Dupré and contributions from Jeff Deyo, Sean Feucht, Julie Meyer, and Rachel Goll Tucker)

Living a Supernatural Life

Passionate Pursuit

Prayer Storm

Praying for Israel's Destiny

The Prophetic Intercessor

A Radical Faith

Releasing Spiritual Gifts Today

The Seer

Shifting Shadows of Supernatural Experiences (with Julia Loren)

Women on the Frontlines series: *A Call to Compassion, A Call to Courage,* and *A Call to the Secret Place* (Michal Ann Goll with James W. Goll)

End Notes

1. Judson W. VanDeVenter, "I Surrender All", (Public Domain, 1896)
2. Paul Baloche, "Open the eyes of my heart, Lord", (Admin. Hal Leonard Publishing Corp., 1997)
3. C. Austin Miles, "I Come to the Garden Alone", (Public Domain, 1913)
4. Bill Gaither, "He Touched Me", (William J. Gaither, 1963)
5. Louisa M. R. Stead "Tis So Sweet to Trust in Jesus", (Public Domain, 1882)
6. Derek Prince, *How to Expel Demons, Break Curses and Release Blessings*, (Chosen Books, 2006)
7. Derek Prince, *From Curse to Blessing*, (Derek Prince Ministries, 1986)
8. For more on these subjects see my book and study guide on *Deliverance from Darkness*.
9. Jonathan David & Melissa Helser, "No Longer Slaves", (Bethel Music Publishing, 2014)
10. Francis Frangipane, *Discerning of Spirits*, (Arrow Publications, 1994)
11. Dr. Michael Brown, *Let No One Deceive You*, p. 61, (Shippensburg, PA: Revival Press, 1997)
12. Fanny Crosby, "Rescue the perishing, care for the dying", (Public Domain, 1869)
13. Rick Joyner, *Overcoming Evil in the Last Days*, p. 130 (Shippensburg, PA: Destiny Image, 2003)
14. Francis Frangipane, *Three Battlegrounds*, (Advancing Church Publication, 1989)
15. James W. Goll, *Prayers that Strike the Mark Study Guide*, (God Encounters Ministries, 2015)
16. Michael Ledner, "You are my hiding place", (Maranatha! Music, 1981)
17. Rick Joyner, *Overcoming Evil in the Last Days*, p. 75, (Shippensburg, PA: Destiny Image, 2003)
18. John Bevere, *The Bait of Satan*, p. 6-7, (Charisma House, Lake Mary FL, 2014)
19. James W. Goll, *Deliverance from Darkness Study Guide*, p.61, (God Encounters Ministries, 2014)
20. James W. Goll, *Deliverance from Darkness Study Guide*, p.65, (God Encounters Ministries, 2014)
21. James W. Goll, *Deliverance from Darkness Study Guide*, p.65, (God Encounters Ministries, 2014)
22. John Bevere, *The Bait of Satan*, p. 6-7, (Charisma House, Lake Mary FL, 2014)
23. Fanny Crosby, "Draw Me Nearer", (Public Domain, 1875)
24. James W. Goll, *Deliverance from Darkness Study Guide*, p.65, (God Encounters Ministries, 2014)
25. Bill Johnson, *Dreaming with God*, (Shippensburg, PA: Destiny Image, 2006)
26. Bill Johnson, *God Is Good*, (Shippensburg, PA: Destiny Image, 2016)
27. Fanny Crosby, "Blessed Assurance", (Public Domain)
28. Martin Luther, "Mighty Fortress is Our God", (Public Domain, 1552)

About the Author

Dr. James W. Goll is the President of God Encounters Ministries, formerly known as Encounters Network, and has founded numerous ministries including Prayer Storm and Women on the Frontlines. He is a member of the Harvest International Ministries apostolic team and an instructor in the Wagner Leadership Institute and Christian Leadership University.

With great joy James has shared Jesus in more than 50 nations teaching and imparting the power of intercession, prophetic ministry, and life in the Spirit.

James is the prolific author of numerous books including *The Seer, The Lost Art of Intercession, The Coming Israel Awakening, Finding Hope,* and the award winning *The Lifestyle of a Prophet*. He has recorded multiple classes with corresponding study guides and full curriculum kits.

In the spirit of revival and reformation, James desires to facilitate unity in body of Christ by relationally networking with leaders of various denominational streams. His passion is to "win for the Lamb the rewards of His suffering." Praying for Israel is a burden of his heart, as Israel fulfills her role in the consummation of the ages.

James and Michal Ann were married for 32 years before her graduation to heaven in the fall of 2008. James has four adult children who are all married: Justin, GraceAnn, Tyler, and Rachel and a growing number of grandchildren. James makes his home in the rolling hills of Franklin, TN.

For More Information & Additional Resources:

James W. Goll
God Encounters Ministries
P.O. Box 1653
Franklin, TN 37065
Visit: www.GodEncounters.com or www.JamesGoll.com

Email: info@godencounters.com
Speaking Invitations: InviteJames@godencounters.com

Additional Resources by James W. Goll

Many of these books feature a corresponding curriculum with a study guide and class taught by James W. Goll, available at www.GodEncounters.com.

Adventures in the Prophetic (with Michal Ann Goll, Mickey Robinson, Patricia King, Jeff Jansen, and Ryan Wyatt)

Angelic Encounters (with Michal Ann Goll)

The Call to the Elijah Revolution (with Lou Engle)

The Coming Israel Awakening

Deliverance from Darkness

The Discerner

Dream Language (with Michal Ann Goll)

Exploring Your Dreams and Visions

Finding Hope

God Encounters Today (with Michal Ann Goll)

Hearing God's Voice Today

The Lifestyle of a Prophet

The Lifestyle of a Watchman

The Lost Art of Intercession

The Lost Art of Practicing His Presence

The Lost Art of Pure Worship (with Chris Dupré and contributions from Jeff Deyo, Sean Feucht, Julie Meyer, and Rachel Goll Tucker)

Living a Supernatural Life

Passionate Pursuit

Prayer Storm

Praying for Israel's Destiny

The Prophetic Intercessor

A Radical Faith

Releasing Spiritual Gifts Today

The Seer

Shifting Shadows of Supernatural Experiences (with Julia Loren)

Women on the Frontlines series: *A Call to Compassion, A Call to Courage,* and *A Call to the Secret Place* (Michal Ann Goll with James W. Goll)

GOD ENCOUNTERS MINISTRIES
with James W. Goll

God Encounters Ministries started around twenty-five years ago in Missouri, originally called Ministry to the Nations. It was a natural - supernatural overflow of the relationship that James and Michal Ann Goll had with Jesus and each other. After moving to the Nashville, TN area in 1996, the ministry was renamed Encounters Network. Through the years the heart and core values of the ministry have remained exactly the same!

Now we are reaching more people than ever with the gospel of Jesus, teaching and imparting the power of prophetic ministry, intercession and life in the Spirit. We believe that God Encounters are for everyone! So visit our website and deepen your walk with God today!

For more info, visit: **GodEncounters.com**

Blog
Grow in your relationship with God. Enjoy poignant articles from James W. Goll that will inspire you.

Classes
18 Online Classes by James W. Goll. Great for self-study or to facilitate a small group in your home or church.

Media
Hundreds of FREE Audio and Video messages ready to revitalize you and give you hope! Access on demand.

Store
Cultivate revelation in your walk of faith. Dynamic resources to equip you and light your spiritual fire.

GOD
ENCOUNTERS
MINISTRIES
with James W. Goll

Made in the USA
Middletown, DE
26 July 2018